When was the last time you tried to punch a hole in the sky?

Tests pilots, punching into stratosphere, climbing to undreamt heights in jets and rocket planes, have a phrase they use to describe their work. They call it 'punching holes in the sky.'

That is what we are meant to do with our lives, to climb beyond the humdrum, to reach beyond the preoccupation of daily existence. However, more often than not, we aim too low. We are human, we tell ourselves. The sky is too high to think of punching holes in it. It is the impossible that stops us. But nonetheless it is the challenge of the impossible that gets life out of its rut and onto a highway that leads us to our goal.

Think big, work hard and have the courage to dream. Concentrate on achieving that dream. *Remember, if you don't care for your dreams, who will.*

Make the impossible your goal. Success begins to happen when you change your 'I can't' philosophy to 'I can'.

Also in
Orient Paperbacks

10 Steps to Positive Living
How to be Your Own Best Friend
Mental Fitness: Exercises to Improve Your Brain Power
Reaching Your Potential
Achieve Success and Happiness

Success in 30 Days
Success is Never Ending, Failure is Never Final!

SECRETS OF SUCCESS

Realise your dreams.
Discover the exciting life of
success and achievement.

Charles Newton

ISBN : 978-81-222-0005-8

Secrets of Success

Subject: Self-Help/Personal Growth

This Printing 2026

Published by
Orient Paperbacks
(A division of Vision Books Pvt. Ltd.)
5 A/8 Ansari Road, New Delhi-110 002
www.orientpaperbacks.com

Cover design by A.R. Designz

Printed and bound at TACT Printers, New Delhi

Contents

1

Passports to Success: Commonsense plus Industry

'Success is most enjoyable when it has been won against odds.'
An Ancient Chinese Proverb

In his delightful short story, *The Verger,* Somerset Maugham describes how a seemingly insoluble problem can be a blessing in disguise. John Smith (I forget the correct name) was employed as a verger in a church in England. The duties of a verger are very simple, such as conducting people to their seats.

One day, the pastor of the church passed an order that all employees must be literate and those who were not must become so by a certain date. When the deadline ended, the pastor sent for John Smith and asked him if he had become literate. When the verger said he was still illiterate, his services were terminated immediately after paying him all his dues, including the balance to his credit in his provident fund account.

Being a crucial day in his life, Smith wanted a cigarette, but could find no tobacconist's booth nearby. That predicament made him think: surely he was not the only one who was so badly in need of a cigarette. With some of his savings, he at once set up a tobacconist's booth. Soon, he had a chain of such booths at strategic points all over London.

One day, the manager of the bank at which Smith had a savings account, sent for him and asked if he knew his bank balance (which had grown to a considerable figure, and the manager wanted to suggest how it could be invested profitably). When Smith said he did not know what his balance was, the manager was astonished because he said statements of account were being posted to Smith regularly. Smith admitted that he was receiving some communications from the bank, but confessed that he could not read.

That confession astounded the manager, who exclaimed: 'Good heavens, man, can you imagine what you'd have been if you could read?'

Smith replied simply: 'Yes, a verger'.

Commonsense is indeed an important key to success. People may have a number of university degrees behind their names, but if they lack commonsense, they remain academic robots all through life.

Commonsense helps us to solve simple problems in life easily. In the process, we progress and eventually attain success.

Congreve says:

'Delay not till tomorrow to be wise;
    Tomorrow's sun to thee may never rise.'

According to R. Collyer, 'A man's best friends are his ten fingers'.

Commonsense tells us that when there is an obstacle in our path, the best way to get past it is to go round, or over it.

Commonsense refuses to allow us to be daunted by adversity or any roadblock. It tells us that if one method for doing something does not succeed, try another. What is the use of high academic qualifications if we cannot apply our knowledge for the solution of simple, everyday problems? And what is the use of commonsense if we do not have the industry to act in accordance with its dictates.

Henry Ward Beecher says: 'In the ordinary business of life, industry can do anything which genius can do, and very many things which it cannot'. In other words, everybody does not have to be a genius to work hard and attain prosperity. This fact is endorsed by Dickens in *Barnaby Rudge,* where he says: 'Industry is the soul of business and the keystone of prosperity'. Procrastination is our deadliest enemy. We should never put off anything till tomorrow what should, and can, be done today.

Generally, artists are thought to be temperamentally lazy, but even so great a painter as Sir Joshua Reynolds says: 'If you have great talents, industry will improve them; if you have but moderate abilities, industry will supply their deficiencies'.

Of course, industry has to be employed in the right channels.

In his *Memoirs,* Field-marshal Lord Montgomery quotes a modern German General as saying: 'I divide my officers into four classes, the clever, the stupid, the industrious, and the lazy. Every officer possesses at least two of those qualities. Those who are clever and industrious are fitted for higher staff appointments; use can be made of those who are stupid and lazy. The man who is clever and lazy is fitted for the highest command; he has the temperament and the requisite nerve to deal with all situations. But whoever is stupid and industrious is a danger and must be removed immediately'.

Commonsense combined with industry can carry us to unimagined heights of success. However, what should be eschewed is undue sensitivity. The further we progress in life, we learn that we have to be thick-skinned—in fact, truly pachydermatous. Indians, in general, are inclined to be too easily hurt and their sensitivity wounded. Taunts and slurs and insults act as spurs and prod us on.

Loss of temper is surely a luxury people in India can ill afford. Lost tempers lead to hot words. Hot words lead to violence. Violence has a variety of forms. Apart from flying at one another's throats, people tend to use whatever implements are handy as weapons of offence—and defence. Easy access to knives, steel rods, and sharp metallic implements results in murder. If the antagonists belong to different ethnic communities, or profess different religions, a communal riot soon breaks out, resulting in heavy loss of life and public property.

A lot of people have a low flash-point. The more civilized a people, the higher is the flash-point. This is because it is easier for the more civilized man to see the other man's point of view. Disputes arise because of misunderstanding. The more understanding a man, the easier is it for him to keep his temper in check. In a dispute, both sides are partly right and partly wrong. A dispute arises because both parties think they are absolutely right and the other side is absolutely wrong. If that was true, there could be no dispute unless one or both parties were mentally unsound.

There is a tendency to use abusive words even when there is no provocation. Most of us use such words as a sort of verbal excretion. As we all know, any excretory function gives pleasure. Many so-called abusive words are really swear-words and therefore innocuous. In earlier days, it used to be common to reinforce a statement by swearing 'on my father', 'on God' and so on. In England, before King Henry VIII severed relations with the Pope in Rome, and the country was still Roman Catholic, it was not unusual for people to swear by the Virgin Mary, commonly referred to as 'Our Lady'. Some people would try to back up an affirmation by saying 'By the blood of our Lady'. This oath was soon contracted to a portmanteau word, 'bloody'. Now the word is regarded as an abuse, even though it has a religious origin and is harmless.

It is true that people in India are unduly sensitive. For this reason, when the country was under British rule, British military officers were given strict instructions not to use the usual military swear-words to Indian officers and other ranks. However, British ranks were subjected to extremely foul language, which they took in their stride. They knew that the seemingly offensive words were not to be interpreted literally.

There is a general acceptance that harsh words break no bones. Moreover, aspersions on the legitimacy of our birth are not meant to be taken seriously. We know that when somebody calls us 'bastard', he cannot transform our birth into an illegitimate one.

We would lose our temper less frequently if we learnt to put ourselves in the offending person's shoes more often.

Usually, the less civilized one is, the greater is his need to resort to verbal excretion in the form of abuse. When we ascend in civilization, we learn to discipline our bodies, minds and speech and stand in less need to utter abuse merely to relieve the mind.

If all of us kept our tempers in check, there would be fewer riots in the country and public property would be more abundant. The man who loses his temper also loses his rationality, and is clearly the loser in a dispute.

It may not be possible to go through life without ever losing our temper, but those who know how to keep the temper firmly in check certainly live longer.

In these days of frequent power cuts, shortage of basic necessities and the problems of commuting to work in large cities in overcrowded public transport vehicles, provocations are very great indeed. But by losing our temper, we are merely in a little worse state than before.

Prestige, too, is inclined to be easily impaired. Far too many people are worried about sullying the family escutcheon. Labour is looked down upon and white-collar jobs favoured. There is definitely no indignity in any form of labour. In contrast, what should be looked down upon is the tendency to beg and to sponge on friends and relatives.

Work done is worship. No truly successful man or woman has ever been a shirker, or excessively concerned about his or her sensitivity.

It is work and not birth that governs the aristocracy of present times.

2

Positive Thinking: The Vision of Success

'All that we are is the result of what we have thought.'

Dhammapada

If we have to go from Kolkata to Delhi, we have to decide on the mode of travel—should we go by road, or by rail, or by air?—and, having come to a firm decision, we have to make the relevant arrangements. Whatever mode of travel we choose, we assume we shall reach our destination speedily and safely. We are not assailed by doubts: Will the car break down on the way? Will the train be derailed? Will our plane crash?

Similarly, when we draw up plans for a career, or for the launching of a new project, we should make a rough 'feasibility report' and assure ourselves that we have the right equipment. We should take 'fair weather' for granted. If we begin listing possible perils on, the way, we stand in danger of getting bogged down at the starting point itself, without any hope of progress. As they rightly say, never venture, never win; no risk, no gain; and fortune favours the brave.

Supposing a boy or girl is interested in the science stream and does well in these subjects at school, after completing school, he or she opts for science at college, and after graduating from there, enrols at a medical college. There is nothing wrong about these decisions because a medical career offers scope for success. There is plenty of room in the world for the intelligent medical graduate in some field or other.

There may not be jobs for everybody, but that does not mean that it is not possible for everybody to be gainfully employed. One can be self-employed. As a developing country, India offers almost unlimited scope for self-employment. If one does not succeed in finding employment within a reasonable period, it does not mean that all hope is lost. Instead, one should be able to think of some simple line of self-employment like offering tuition to the extent of one's capacity, or cashing in on any talent like singing, or drawing, or acumen with a camera, till one finds the right opening in the realm of full-time employment.

Timidity and fear are great obstacles to progress. Why should we set up road blocks in our own path by imagining all sorts of dangers? Bridges should be crossed only when we come to them. It is only the stupid and the timid who want to cross imaginary bridges long before reaching them.

As James Allen says: 'Dream lofty dreams, and as you dream so shall you become. Your vision is the promise of what you shall one day be; your ideal is the prophecy of what you shall at last unveil. Your circumstances may be uncongenial, but they shall not long remain so if you perceive an ideal and strive to reach it.

Most people imagine that it is essential to be a bookworm to be successful. There was a Jewish couple in England some years ago who set their hearts on having a son. When a son was born to them, they were insistent that he should be a genius. His record at school, however, dismayed his parents, who had to employ a number of tutors to help the boy scrape through his examinations from one class to the next. After completing school with the greatest of difficulty, the boy was sent to Oxford, where he did not fare any better. To avoid any discrimination, the family changed its name from a typically Jewish one to Abercrombie.

One day, Mr and Mrs Abercrombie went to Wembley Station in London to see a football match between England and Scotland. Their son was playing for England and the stadium was a sea of heads. Suddenly, the game progressed, the spectators were so excited that they stood up and shouted in unison, 'Abercrombie's got the ball, Abercrombie's got the ball, Abercrombie is a genius'.

Mr and Mrs Abercrombie were absolutely dazed. All these years, they had been spending a large amount of money on private tutors for their son in the hope that he would be transformed into a genius. Excitement in a crowd being contagious, they too stood up along with the others and yelled, 'Abercrombie's got the ball, Abercrombie's got the ball, Abercrombie is a genius!'

So their problem son was indeed a genius—but far removed from the kind of genius they had visualized, or rather from their conception of a genius. A prime essential for success in any walk of life is robust commonsense. Whatever one sets out to do—assuming that it is worth doing—should be done in the firm belief that one will succeed. As they say, when we strive for the Moon, we just skim the tops of the trees. In other words, we have to have firm faith in the virtues of our object, and, next, firm faith in ourselves. Hoary maxims like 'God helps those who help themselves' are not empty words, but facts that have been tested and parts of experience.

We have to disabuse our minds of myths, fetishes and old wives' tales. When we observe those who have succeeded in some field, we find that they do not wait for a particular time of day to do something, but do as much as they can during their working hours, usually abnormally long. They do not wait for a lucky day on which to attempt something important, but plunge themselves into it at the first opportunity. They do not consult astrologers and palmists to ascertain 'favourable' and 'unfavourable' periods, but treat all periods alike.

As Napoleon Bonaparte rightly said, 'The truest wisdom, in general, is a resolute determination'. Indecision, uncertainty, and lack of faith in our competence are fatal weaknesses. Every step has to be planned carefully and taken with supreme confidence.

3

The Importance of Concentration

> *'The true, strong, and sound mind is the mind that carries man afar.'*
>
> Anonymous

Lloyd George was once asked. 'To what do you attribute your greatness?' He replied laconically: 'When I brush my hair, I think of nothing else but brushing my hair'.

That sort of intensity is extremely important for success. The ability to concentrate is the mark of a disciplined and orderly mind. Unhappily, what plagues administration in India most is the general and shocking inability to concentrate on the job. This 'grasshopper mind' results in incompetence and heavy loss of time.

Even the highest officers have a habit of conferring with visitors in the presence of a medley of clerks and other junior functionaries. There is a constant, unregulated traffic in and out of officers' rooms, irrespective of the status of visitors who may be present and the importance of their conversation, or the essentiality of its privacy. Cabinet Ministers and others of corresponding status, too, are constantly surrounded by diverse retainers and other personnel when visitors call on them for important discussions. When Stalin's daughter, Svetlana Allulieva, was in India with the object of seeking political asylum, she complained that she was never able to have a few words with the Prime Minister, Mrs Indira Gandhi, in complete privacy.

It appears that Indian officers have an inherent habit of talking to people 'in public', or collectively. The age-old practice of the country's rulers to hold *durbars,* or to give *darshan* to their subjects might have influenced them.

Whatever may be the origin of 'open' conferences, it ought to be obvious now that they serve hardly any purpose, are a waste of precious time, and highly insulting to the people concerned. It would be better not to see an official visitor at all if an officer does not have the time to see him in privacy than to see him in the presence of strangers, before whom he is not able to say all that he may want to say.

No officer, whether in the Government or in a business house, should be so busy that his privacy is constantly invaded by members of his staff or by outsiders. It should not be difficult to regulate the flow of visitors, whether internal or external, with the help of competent secretarial staff. It is merely a lack of efficient regulation that transforms an important officer's room into some sort of a public waiting room. Many Cabinet Ministers and politicians in general like to give the impression that they are easily accessible and truly democratic.

It may be possible for Cabinet Ministers and politicians to address a number of people together with a fair measure of attentiveness. This feat is certainly beyond the competence of the office executives. Nevertheless, most officers' rooms are open to the public to walk in whenever they like. Sometimes, an officer may be in the midst of an important conversation with a visitor when another caller arrives. Immediately, the officer interrupts his conversation with the earlier visitor and turns his attention to the latter one. Then he keeps alternating between the two.

Surely, it should not be too difficult for the officer to appreciate the wisdom of talking to one visitor at a time and of concentrating his attention on one job. This practice would ensure greater satisfaction for all concerned, result in a higher level of efficiency and reduce loss of time.

In some of the smaller proprietary concerns, the chief executive's room becomes a sort of club, which is open throughout the day to his unemployed or less employed friends. We can well imagine the amount of serious work that is possible in this state of affairs. Must friends be entertained at offices during working hours? What opinion must clerks and other employees hold of such ill-disciplined employers?

Sometimes, officers in the midst of important conferences are called on the telephone by near relatives or friends for a conversation that could have well been reserved for after-office hours. When Mr Richard Nixon was President of the USA, he was once presiding over a Cabinet meeting when the telephone rang and he broke off to hold a long and intimate conversation. As soon as it ended, he apologized to his colleagues, explaining with an indulgent smile: 'That was Julie (his daughter). She wanted to know the issues involved in Vietnam'. In principle, that sort of intrusion is quite wrong and cannot be justified even if the offender happens to be the daughter of the President of the USA.

Of course, emergencies are exceptions and one cannot be inhuman about them. But, happily, they are rare and not everyday features.

Clearly, officers and others in responsible positions should severely discourage telephone calls and visits by relatives and friends during working hours. After all, a telephone call can be wrongly handled and result in embarrassment, as it did on one occasion for the manager of a business house. He asked his assistant to take the call, but the junior promptly handed the receiver to the manager, saying, 'Sorry sir, it's your wife'. When asked why he thought so, the assistant said: 'As soon as I said, "Hello", a lady at the other end rasped: "Is that you, you old fool?" '

4

Begin at the Bottom

'Who guards his post, no matter where,
Believing God must need him there.
Although but lowly toil it be,
Has risen to nobility.'

Edgar A. Guest

Some industrial and commercial magnates are chary of allowing their sons to work in junior positions, in the mistaken belief that this procedure would be demeaning for their precious offspring. In sharp contrast, however, giants such as Ford and Rockefeller insisted that their sons begin life in the family organizations as common workmen—and even then, subject to much stricter discipline than their colleagues. Promotion depended strictly on merit and the yardstick for merit was harsher than that applied to workers in general.

By beginning at the top, business executives are totally ignorant of what happens at the bottom and at other levels in the organization, and in consequence remain at the mercy of their employees. Moreover, because of lack of this detailed knowledge of operations at every level, the whole set-up tends to be inefficient and loose-knit. As a result, other undesirable features, such as wastage, dishonesty and petty larceny, develop and continue unchecked, with disastrous economic consequences.

On the other hand, in the West, business and other executives study every aspect of the working of an organization before assuming administrative control, and it helps in identifying any lapse or deficiency and rectifying it. As a result of the firm control over all personnel, their work and shortcomings, Western organizations are comparatively efficient and streamlined.

Many young men launch into business straight after leaving school or college, without any prior knowledge of the venture. For instance, numerous people attempt to publish journals without any practical experience of journalism. But Lord Northcliffe, famous as 'the Napoleon of the Press', who, by the time he died, was at the head of a vast publishing empire, comprising 110 newspapers and magazines, including the greatest paper in the English-speaking world at that time, *The Times*, with a total circulation of 55 million, began life as a compositor and hawker. So powerful was Northcliffe at the peak of his career that he could make and break Governments just as children make and break sand castles. He forced Asquith to resign as Prime Minister during the First World War and brought in Lloyd George who used to consult the Press Baron before presenting his Budget.

Similarly, a young man in the USA who wanted to manufacture electronic computers, first made a thorough study of the science of cybernetics. Not astonishingly, his concern is now a multi-million-dollar business, employing a few thousand personnel, and growing rapidly.

Oddly, as soon as boys leave school or college, their parents present these young men a business project, or the capital for setting up one, so that they can busy themselves with a hobby, in the same way as parents in the West buy their bright young ones a toy train.

For instance, a wealthy business man recently, gave his son, who had just passed out from a famous public school, ample funds with which to launch a monthly magazine. This young man's only qualification in 'journalism' was that he had contributed to his school magazine and had also produced a small journal for private circulation as a hobby. With the loftiest self-confidence in his writing ability and in the prolificity of his brain-waves, he offered contributors a fairly lavish rate of payment to write for a journal that had still to find its feet. But, sadly, only a year or so later, inquiry revealed that his 'baby' had breathed its last, after incurring a staggering loss.

Those who enter Government service or some other form of administrative work would be equally well advised to study the entire structure of their offices before ensconcing themselves in the luxury of an air-conditioned sanctum. It is true that some of the larger organizations in the private sector encourage young officers to go through what is known as an 'induction course', but, by and large, people who begin life in the executive cadres tend to look down upon those in the worker or clerical ones.

It can safely be said that the wider and deeper his experience, the better will an administrator be. Obviously, it is safe and wise to know all the ground under our feet, rather than to be transplanted suddenly on alien soil. And is it not better to climb a staircase one step at a time, rather than attempt to reach the top in one leap?

5

Of Leaders and Followers

'I must follow them; I am their leader.'

Andrew Bonar Law

There are only two kinds of people in the world—those who lead and those who follow. Therefore each one of us has to decide in which category he or she would like to be. However, it is not merely a question of our likes, but one of aptitude, potential and determination as well. After all, everybody cannot be an Alexander the Great, or a Julius Caesar or a Napoleon Bonaparte or a Mahatma Gandhi, merely by wishing he were so. Much depends on our capacity and the field for which it is best qualified. Leadership is a relative term and not limited only to those who rise to world dominance, or even to national greatness in the political sphere. Doesn't a football, or a hockey team have a leader?

There is hardly any sphere of life in which a leader is not required. And whereas very few of us dream of being a Jawaharlal Nehru or a Mahatma Gandhi, most of us do have sound and legitimate hopes of success in our profession or in whatever career we choose.

But the trouble is that very few of us are daring and courageous enough to risk unpopularity by departing from the 'herd'. By far the safest and commonest course appears to be: 'Follow the leader'. Among a group of friends, if the most popular member says that A is the best film showing in town that week, all will readily concur, even if another member is convinced that that is not so. But he sinks his individuality and thinks it would be safer to go along with the crowd rather than be stigmatized as a 'square' or an 'odd man out'.

That is precisely where our powers of leadership come in. Do we have the courage to say, 'No', when all around us are united in a loud chorus of 'Yes'? Ibsen says: 'The strongest man in the world is he who stands most alone'.

Timidity leads us into committing the most appalling blunders. When somebody in a group is discussing a book, and one of the members has not read it, he does not have the courage to confess his ignorance. At the same time, in the effort to be 'in', he makes such statements that his stupidity is exposed and all respect for him lost. An attractive young woman once found herself seated next to Winston Churchill at a party. Thinking she would impress the famous statesman not only with her looks but with her intelligence as well, she began a discussion on books. Churchill eyed her suspiciously and asked if she had read Scott's *The Talisman*. 'Of course, it's wonderful', came the gushing reply.

'Have you read Scott's *Ivanhoe*?'

'Rather', came the ecstatic reply, 'it's superb'.

'And what about Scott's *Emulsion*?' Churchill asked impishly.

'O, I think that's his best work by far', sighed the poor innocent.

This tendency, unfortunately, is all too common all over the country in general. In consequence, there is the distressing spectacle of a lamentable lack of leadership of any consequence, and almost total absence of even executive ability. As is well known, what India needs most today is managerial and executive talent or, in other words, group leaders.

The country's present devastating famine in the realm of executive ability stems simply from the fear of taking decisions. And yet the ability to make a spot decision is what differentiates the executive, or leader, from the clerk.

In an article in *Weekly Scotsman*, Sheila Gould says: 'Working for a vast industrial concern, as I do, one gets a chance to observe tycoons at close quarters and they probably all have one thing in common—the ability to make the decision, stand by it, and not to blame anyone else but themselves if anything goes wrong. . . . What makes a tycoon tick? The three important things which stood out in my mind are amazing energy, the kind that can go 24 hours without sleep, the ability to make a decision instantly, and, above all else, the attention to detail'.

Remember that when your advice is asked, you mustn't say what you know to be popular but wrong. You must say what you think is right—provided of course you are dead sure-even though you may court momentary unpleasantness. That momentary unpleasantness will assuredly be transformed into deep and lasting respect for you, once you have been proved right.

There is no point in going along with the herd in the belief that that policy ensures happiness and contentment. If you are happy and contented so easily, you cannot expect much success in life. As Napoleon wrote to General Lauriston in 1804: 'Death is nothing, but to live defeated and inglorious is to die daily'.

In life we have to take bold decisions and take them quickly. The weak, the timorous and the undecided are swept aside by the tide of events. Once we choose a career, or a profession, we have to equip ourselves for it, and once we are launched on our chosen course, we have to see that we reach the top somehow. For those who try, this is not difficult. There have been cases in India—not many, alas—of postmen who have retired as Postmasters General; of humble police constables who have ended their careers as Inspector-General of police; and there is the example of the late Mr. V.P. Menon, who began life as a Division III clerk in the Imperial Secretariat in New Delhi, but rose dramatically to become Secretary of the Ministry of States, when it was headed by Sardar Vallabhbhai Patel. It was Mr Menon who worked out all the details of the integration of the princely States in the Indian Union, and eventually became Governor of Kerala.

With courage and determination, only the sky is the limit!

6

Learn from the Great

'Lives of great men all remind us
We can make our lives sublime,
And, departing, leave behind us
Footprints on the sands of time.'

H.W. Longfellow

People who distinguish themselves in any walk of life should be admired, but not worshipped. They may have specialized in one or more lines but their success in these specialities does not mean that they are infallible in whatever they do.

When some people surpass in any field it does not necessarily mean that these heroes and heroines are super-human beings. These celebrities tower above the rest around them because the others are sub-standard. Vanity prevents us from admitting that we are sub-standard. We flatter ourselves when we promote ourselves to the standard level. Naturally, when we believe that we belong to the standard level, those above this level are thought to be super-standard, or super-men and super-women.

Concentration and determination can enable us to attain success in any field. Everyone cannot become an Einstein or a William Shakespeare. Everybody does not have that aspiration.

Each one of us has a certain aptitude. We should try and develop ourselves in consonance with our latent ability and talent. Only a fool of a man with an aptitude for painting would try to attain the heights of Edison or Marconi. As a result of diligence, dogged perseverance, determination, and single-minded devotion, he would not be so far off the mark if he tried to reach the level of Renoir or Gauguin.

Every specialist attains distinction of a certain level. Those who attain an unsurpassed level are said to be great—great in a specialized field. Strangely, the general masses mistake this specialized distinction to be 'super-human' greatness.

Recently, some friends of mine were ecstatic in their admiration of journalists. They said that journalists were 'great people' because they conversed with such luminaries as kings, presidents, prime ministers and other dignitaries. I reminded these friends that if kings and prime ministers agreed to converse with journalists, it was simply because of official expediency—to earn publicity for themselves and their views. After all, kings and prime ministers talk to their domestic staff as well and perhaps on points of greater intimacy than are discussed with journalists. Therefore, by the same yardstick, cooks and bearers, too, should be 'great people'.

If we put everything in proper perspective, we are not likely to be so easily overwhelmed and knocked off our balance. In his *Autobiography*, Charlie Chaplin rightly says: 'I found poverty neither attractive nor edifying. It taught me nothing but a distortion of values, on over-rating of the virtues and graces of the rich and so-called better classes.

'Wealth and celebrity, on the contrary, taught me to view the world in proper perspective, to discover that men of eminence, when I came close to them, were as deficient in their way as the rest of us.'

All of us cannot sweep a public road with as much competence as a professional sweeper, nor can we shine a pair of shoes with the same virtuosity as the skilled roadside shoeshine. But though the sweeper and the shoeshine surpass us in their respective trades, it cannot be said that they are greater humans in general than the rest of us.

Regrettably, we tend to deify great men and women and wrongly assume that we can never equal their virtues. When we read the lives of the world's greatest men and women, we find that at the outset, they were just like all of us. But, unlike us, they did not worship their great predecessors; nor were they paralysed by the conviction that they could never dream of attaining such heights. On the other hand, they were inspired and stimulated by the deeds of the celebrities of earlier days, and resolved to emulate them.

Blind hero worship merely tends to stunt intellectual growth. We are inclined to magnify the virtues of our 'heroes' and to minimize our own. As a result we widen the gulf between our 'heroes' and ourselves. When this happens on a large scale, the 'heroes' begin to have an inflated opinion of their capability and achievements and look down on their blind admirers with corresponding contempt. It is this attitude that led to the dominance of men such as Hitler and Mussolini, who transformed themselves into dictatorial tyrants. In earlier days, this same attitude led despots to usurp royal prerogatives and to describe their acts as 'the divine right of kings'.

In India, the masses tend to worship Mahatma Gandhi and Jawaharlal Nehru with equal blindness, without making any effort to imbibe the ideals of these great leaders.

Instead of worshipping 'heroes' in blind admiration, we would do well to analyse the aspects of their greatness and try to adopt them as far as practicable in our own lives. By adoring our 'heroes', we cannot hope to be like them we shall always be what we are. It is only by trying to do what our 'heroes' have done that we have a chance of rising to some extent above over present level and attaining a modicum of success.

7

School Never Ends

'The things taught in schools and colleges are not an education but the means of education.'

Emerson

Many pupils mistakenly think they leave school behind for good the day they pass the Matriculation, or the School Leaving Certificate, examination. But in fact we never finish with school so long as we breathe. Or to put it another way, life is one endless school session.

Most of the good schools at best are preparatory institutions. They help us to build a rudimentary foundation on which we ourselves have to erect the superstructure of knowledge. A School Leaving Certificate may be a passport to life no doubt, but, having earned it, we may not be well groomed enough to begin life. We might have emerged from our chrysalis, but our edges show only too painfully the moment we begin to rub up against fellow adults. Soon, we discover that a vital component of education, left untouched by our school curriculum, has still to be learnt, and learnt fast, if we wish to make a success of our lives. That missing component can be described best as public relations, or the art of getting along with our fellow beings.

So important is public relations in the various spheres of life that an increasing number of business houses and public institutions have special departments to take care of this vital requirement. It is the object of the public relations organization to project a certain image—obviously as pleasing as possible—of the institution it represents in the public mind. For instance, when we mention the name of a manufactured product, such as a soap or a toothpaste, what picture does the listener at once form in his or her mind? Is it of a pleasant object, or an unpleasant one? Does it bring to mind pleasant associations with that particular name, or unpleasant ones?

Every public relations organization strives to build the best possible image of the product, or products, it represents, so must we, in our individual lives, strive to build the best possible image in the public mind for ourselves.

But we begin with a disadvantage—we have to be our own Public Relations Officers, in addition to whatever position we may hold for earning a livelihood.

Our first object should be to smoothen some of our rough edges, so as to make ourselves acceptable socially on as wide a scale as possible. Obviously, we are too young and immature when we are at conventional high schools to know much about the complexities of human nature. And knowledge of human nature is important if we wish to save ourselves from social jolts, and bumps, and bruises.

One of the first lessons we learn is that adults are much more conscious of general appearance, conduct, and social armour than children. They are also much more sensitive than children about any chinks in 'facade', so to say.

All that glitters may not to be gold, but it is certainly something very desirable socially, and therefore gold figuratively. The ancient Romans said: *Mentem hominis spectato non frontem* (I see a man's mind, not the appearance). They had the time and the leisure to think so. We do not. Thus, appearance does count.

Of course, I do not intend to suggest that those of us who do not look like glamorous film stars, or fashion plates, do not have any future. What we have to develop increasingly after we leave conventional schools is discretion. It is this faculty that tells us what is in good taste, and what is not. Nobody can teach us to develop discretion. We learn by trial and error.

It is generally agreed that a tidy appearance—which should not be confused with foppery—is an asset, and helps to open many doors that would otherwise remain closed. Add to that a pleasing voice, and right department, and the overall result produces a very favourable image indeed.

Perhaps, if we had a finishing school after the conventional school course, where we could be taught how to build poise and self-assurance, it would be ideal. As things are, we have to learn *poco a poco*, as the Italians say.

But the tragedy is, as I said at the outset, that we think we know everything and need to learn nothing. If only we could be convinced that we have to learn everything—all over again. That would be the correct starting point.

Unlike reading, (w)riting, and 'rithmetic, how to smoothen our rough edges cannot be learnt from books, but from the hard school of experience. We lose our edges little by little, just as a piece of rock on the seashore loses its edges by being constantly bashed by the waves till it turns into a smooth, round pebble.

8

Importance of Sound Planning

'Strong and organized purposefulness towards a definite objective will focus your powers into a strong motivation in attainment of your goal.'

Leonardo Da Vinci

Since we live only once, and life is short, it behoves us to see that we attain the maximum possible success in whatever we do. Regrettably, far too many people keep taking chances almost throughout life, as though it were some sort of an endless game. After completing school, they enter university, without first thinking of a career and ascertaining whether or not a university degree is absolutely essential, and if it is, the kind of degree required. In many cases, a university degree is not necessary, and those who go through the trouble of acquiring one, merely waste precious time and their parents' money.

At the next stage—that of embarking on a professional career—most young people are not sure in which direction their aptitude lies. Many plump for the first offer of employment, and after that, keep playing a sort of hopscotch with jobs, without making any significant progress in any direction. What is our object in life: is it merely to draw a large salary, irrespective of the work we do and whether or not we have the requisite aptitude for it, and whether or not it sustains our life-long interest? Even when we choose a career for which we are well suited, and which measures up to our interests and inclinations, we have to consider such factors as the extent of competition, the scope for financial and general progress, and whether or not we are strong enough to withstand any occupational hazards.

Moreover, we must also decide as to what kind of progress is best for us—horizontal or vertical. Horizontal progress involves the coverage of a wide area, but we may not rise very high in the professional hierarchy. For example, a journalist may acquire experience of work on the staff of a newspaper, then on that of a magazine, after which he may join a news agency, and, later, a syndicate, without necessarily, rising to be head of any of these organizations. Vertical progress, on the other hand, means that we climb a professional ladder systematically from the bottom rung, step by step, to the top.

Another important decision we have to make concerns the stage at which we should marry. Sometimes, early marriage hampers our professional career, but, in some cases, a successful marriage can be a potent factor in the attainment of rapid success.

Apart from our ability to map out the course of our lives with as great care, perseverance and imagination as possible, we must also see that we do not embark on a major venture of any kind as a result of a sudden whim or impulse. Far too many people wake up at the last minute into the realization that it is their firm's anniversary, and decide to organize a celebration. This sort of eleventh-hour rush results in slipshod organization and the entire celebration, which entails considerable expenditure, turns out to be a loss of prestige and money.

We may happen to be important office-bearers of the executive committee of an association and have to organize a key function of some kind. Here again, the tendency is to delay the completion of major segments of work, with the result that the programme of the grand day turns out to be a fiasco.

Some years ago, I was asked to conduct the publicity campaign for an organization that suddenly decided to hold a 'National Dance Festival'. From the name itself, the project was an unduly ambitious one. A number of committees and sub-committees were set up, with honorary office-bearers totalling at least 150. But so large a contingent of volunteers has to work in close co-ordination, and the director of the entire project must need be a virtual generalissimo. An attendant problem is that too many people want to bask in the glory of being 'office-bearers', but too few have any inclination or competence for actual work. Throughout the three days of the 'Festival', there was a great deal of chaos, which rose to a peak on the last day, when a sudden and unseasonal rain-storm ripped the awning and literally washed out everything. Irate members of the public understandably clamoured for the refund of their money, and the organizers sadly found themselves in heavy debt.

Lamentably, there are far too many ill-planned attempts of this nature, almost every day, resulting in loss of prestige for the organizers and the country as well. It appears that some people wake one fine morning and decide to organize a show, or a celebration of some kind, without counting the cost of the trouble involved. Manifestly, whatever we do, particularly if the public is to be invited to see our effort, should be done free of any flaws. After all, there is little point in undergoing heavy financial expenditure and physical labour only to be ridiculed and to be the victims of opprobrium.

At the other end of the scale, ponder the superb success of the last World Olympic Games, which required years of careful planning in incredibly minute detail.

Whatever we plan, a small birthday party, or a centenary celebration, or a professional symposium, we must see that everything goes off with clockwork precision and that no bad taste is left in anybody's mouth.

Not for nothing does a Chinese proverb says:

'If you are planning for one year, plant grain.
If you are planning for ten years, plant trees.
If you are planning for a hundred years, plant men'.

9

Plan Your Day

> *'When one has much to put into them, a day has a hundred pockets.'*
>
> Freidrich Nietzche

Very few of us fill 'the unforgiving minute with sixty seconds' worth of distance run and these lost seconds add up to lost minutes; lost minutes add up to lost hours; lost hours add up to lost days; lost days add up to lost years; and lost years add up to a fruitless life, or a life in which so much remained undone.

Regrettably, the day is far too short, and there is so much to do if you wish to be a real leader. Many aspirants to leadership—that is to say, office executives, business men, and people in the professions (doctors, teachers, engineers, lawyers, journalists and others)—are content to drift along through the day, because they do not prepare a definite schedule of their activities, and so it is not astonishing that at the end of the day, they find that very little has been achieved. Sadly, this is how day succeeds day, resulting in a life of very little achievement.

Many of us have no fixed time for rising, and so often we sleep extra long, and have to race through the morning newspaper, bath, dress, bolt our breakfast, and hurry along to the office. There, because we have no clear-cut ideas of all that we have to do during the day, we chat over-long to a friend who may call, and sometimes there are many callers, resulting in half-completed work, which is deferred to the next day. If we do not lose time through callers, there are telephone calls, which tend to become unduly protracted, and before we know what is happening, it is time for the office to close. In the evening, we go home and take the family to see a film, or to call on friends, or to go to the club, after which we dine and retire for the night. The day is over, and it consisted mainly of talking, rushing through routine trivia, eating, being entertained, and the dying hours are lost in sleep.

On the other hand, when we discipline ourselves rigidly, prepare a schedule, in advance, of all our activities during the whole day, and ration time in proportion to the importance of different spheres of activity—official work, entertainment and recreation, self-improvement, social and committee duties, meals—we find we can cram much more into a brief span of 24 hours, and enjoy a sense of satisfaction and achievement.

It is best to draw up a schedule for the next day's activities at night. By doing so, we know when exactly we have to rise next morning and at what pace we have to complete the various items on our schedule, so as to conform to it fully. Next day, as we complete each item, we can tick it off, and also see whether or not we are abreast of the time. At work, it would be wise to keep away callers (either in person or on the telephone) who do not have any business to discuss, but are interested in engaging in merely social pleasantries. Obviously, working hours should be reserved for work exclusively, just as during our recreational period we should not give our official worries even a passing thought.

With a schedule to guide us, we are also reminded that even official callers and business talk should be dealt with as much speed as courtesy permits, and we are restrained from digressions and meandering from the basic essentials.

We should be able to set aside a certain amount of time every day for the family, for exercise and wholesome recreation, and for reading and other means of self-improvement. Often, there are instructive and interesting talks by experts at some club or institution, and exhibitions, music recitals and other cultural activities that the intelligent human should not ignore. We might also be taking a course of some kind for improving our professional and general prospects, and of course all aspirants to leadership in any direction should be well-informed individuals, and therefore abreast of human knowledge as far as practicable.

In other words, our work and even recreational activities assume a well-ordered pattern. What we eliminate by following a daily schedule is wastage of time. And in reducing wastage to the very minimum, we fill the day with purposeful activity.

A man, who recently resigned his post in a business house so as to enable him to devote his time to publicity work, confessed to me, with pitiable naivety, that he could never draw up a schedule for the day, because he was convinced that he could not adhere to it rigidly. He stressed with considerable finality that he was just not used to drawing up a schedule. And for that reason, I am not astonished when I see him at street corners, wearing all the appearance of an idler, or a man to whom time means little or nothing.

We have to plan not only our progress as individuals but as leaders of our families, and in the latter capacity, we have to ensure that we give our children the right lead.

Moreover, many of us who are climbing the leadership ladder, are members of various societies, associations and other bodies. As such, we have to attend various committee meetings, and set aside a certain amount of time to pull our due weight in all these organizations, which are important to us in one way or other.

When time is fully utilized to maximum advantage, we are truly impressed with the amount of work that can be done in one day, without tiring ourselves unduly. Of course, all our less systematic friends think that we burn the midnight oil and wonder how we can transform ourselves into veritable demons of energy. But the secret of whatever little success we may enjoy is that we are merely making the most scientific and systematic use of time.

10

Management of Time

'Seize time by the forelock.'

Pittacus of Mitylene

Time is one of our most precious resources. It is also possibly the only one that, once lost, can never be retrieved.

Thus does Longfellow advise:

Look not mournfully into the past
    It returns not again;
Wisely improve the present—it is thine;
    Go forth into the shadowy future
Without fear and a manly heart.

More of us are familiar with Omar Khayyam's lines:

The moving finger writes
    And having writ, moves on;
Not all they piety nor wit

Can lure it back,
Nor all thy tears
Erase one word of it.

Time is indeed remorseless. How wisely do we utilize so invaluable an asset? Roughly, we spend one-third of a lifetime in sleep; a tenth in eating and drinking; another tenth in bathing, tidying ourselves and in the various other minutiae of the toilette. We spend at least a sixth of our lives in chatting with friends, relatives, feeding ourselves and in recreation of diverse varieties. Thus 70 per cent of a lifetime has vanished and only 30 per cent remains—for work.

With a little judicious time management, we could achieve more, attain greater prosperity and make life in general more pleasant for ourselves and our families.

We talk too much. An unconscionably long time is frittered away in idle chatter and gossip. Why cannot we discipline ourselves and slash this heavy waste of time?

Supposing we timed all our actions outside the realm of work. Sleep of course is a basic essential. We repair all our worn-out cells during sleep, which has a rejuvenative, tonic effect. Sleep is Nature's bonus for a hard day's work. Therefore, the harder we work, the more generous is Nature's bonus and the more soundly do we sleep.

But that treasure chest of wisdom, *the Book of Proverbs* in the Bible, advises: 'Love not sleep, lest you come to poverty; open your eyes and you will have plenty of bread'. It says further: 'Go to the ant, O sluggard, consider her ways and be wise. Without having any chief, officer, or ruler, she prepares her food in summer, and gathers her sustenance in harvest. . . Yet a little sleep, a little slumber. A little folding of the hands to sleep, so shall thy poverty come as one that travelleth, and thy want as an armed man'.

But when we rise from bed, why cannot we speed the various actions? The routine of the toilette could be hastened. Breakfast should not take more than 15 to 20 minutes. Everybody does not have to pore over the newspaper excessively. We should drill ourselves in fast reading. Work should begin at 9A.M. at the latest. Lunch could be reduced to half an hour (from 1 to 1:30 P.M.). We should be back at work till 6 P.M. Thus, we would spend 8½ hours a day in concentrated work—or 35 per cent of a lifetime.

Those timings are for the average human. For the more industrious, 10 to 11 hours of work a day would do no harm.

There is no point in over-straining ourselves in the mere attempt to be stakhanovites. We would do well to ponder the parody composed by doctors in the U.K. to Kipling's *If:*

> If you keep filling the unforgiving minute
> With sixty seconds worth of distance run,
> You'll be a coronary before you're fifty-one.

Health is of prime importance for the workaholic. Therefore, diet should be as scientifically nutritious as possible. According to the author of *Wellsprings of Civilization,* who did some research on the role of diet in the progress of civilization, the Sikh diet is best in India and hence the robustness, hardihood and industry of the Sikhs.

Recreation, too, has vitamin value, and it is as important to know how to relax as it is to know how to work.

Far too much time is wantonly wasted. If it had been utilized wisely, we would not be in the morass in which we find ourselves. After 7,000 years or so of so-called civilization, one-sixth of human beings are still illiterate—and India accounts for half the 800 million illiterates in the world—and the average educational level of the world's population is only middle school.

Better utilization of time is dependent on our vitality, which, in its turn, depends on our stamina, and stamina depends on the general state of our health.

Since life is short, so is time. Thus Stephen Grellet said: 'I expect to pass through this world but once. Any good therefore that I can do, or any kindness that I can show to any fellow creature, let me do it now. Let me not defer or neglect it, for I shall not pass this way again'.

Clocks and watches should be venerated—in India in particular, because this country is behind not only the industrialized countries of the West, but also many in Asia itself.

Benjamin Disraeli says, 'He who gains time gains everything'.

Even in the ancient past, Seneca cautioned his readers, 'Note the rapidity of time—that swiftest of things'.

Francis Bacon, too, stresses the importance of time in his *Essays*, when he says: 'Time is the measure of business as money is of wares'.

It would be well to heed Benjamin Franklin's sage counsel: 'Dost thou love life? Then do not squander time, for that's the stuff life is made of'.

And here is Oliver Wendell Holmes's tribute to so priceless an asset:

'Pick my left pocket of its silver dime,
    But spare the right—it holds my golden time!'

11

Value of Effective Communication

'Speech is the index of the mind.'

Seneca

Dale Carnegie very rightly says that no sound is sweeter to our ears than that of our name. This is a cardinal truth and yet it is so widely overlooked and ignored.

Why are human beings in general and Indians in particular so frightened of building personal relations? Correspondence in India—Governmental, business and other varieties—is so impersonal that it tends to be inhuman. Letters give the impression that one robot is writing to another.

Formerly, during the British regime, a letter from a Government officer would begin with the cliche, 'Sir, I have the honour to inform you. . .' and end with the absurd formula, 'I have the honour to be, Sir, your most obedient servant. . .' Happily, the Government of independent India has done away with that archaic and hypocritical form of correspondence.

Business houses, however, which never tire of boasting how many jumps ahead of the Government they are, and of their enterprise and efficiency, still cling to outmoded forms and phrases in letters. Indeed, so well entrenched has commercialise become that it has given birth to English of a distinctive genre—'Business English'—on which a number of books, uniformly entitled, *'How To Write Business Letters'*, are to be found, particularly at the more plebeian types of pavement 'book-stalls'. Because of this stereotyped form of letter-writing, a business letter is just a string of outworn cliches.

Lamentably, people seem to forget that a letter is meant to take the place of conversation. When we speak to one another, do we use the same form and set of words so beloved by letter-writers in commercial establishments?

Although it is well known that public relations and personal contacts have to be built for the promotion of business, many Indian establishments invariably address the party to which they write as 'Sir', even though the same two people may have been in correspondence for years. And just as an officer in business house A appears to be disinterested in knowing the name of the officer in business B, to whom he is writing, he appears to be equally diffident to reveal his own name, judging by the indecipherable signatures at the end of the letter.

As a free-lance, I help to edit and produce a few small publications. Since they are small, they also lack personnel and so I have to draft the more important letters, particularly those concerning the payment of outstanding bills. To draft a letter, naturally I ask for as much data as I can about the party to which I have to write and for previous correspondence with it. Invariably, however, I find that nobody knows the name of the individual at the other end, to whom a letter has to be written. When a letter is addressed officially to, The Manager, XYZ Co., it can be opened not by Mr Singh, the Manager, but by Mr Prasad, his assistant. If the Manager has been reminded about some payment that is overdue, Mr Prasad decides not to disturb his officer, but to pass the letter on to the Accounts Department, which goes to sleep on it.

This antiquated, stilted, Victorian style of correspondence retards business enormously in the country, particularly among the smaller units, which number a few hundred thousand, whereas the streamlined units, number only a few hundred.

Not only should we take the trouble to find out the name of the person to whom we are speaking or writing, but also its correct pronunciation and spelling.

Many names are shared by a number of people, and so the more discerning adopt a distinctive form of spelling to distinguish themselves from namesakes. For instance, Banerjee is spelt Bannerji, Bannerjee, Banerjea, Bannerjea and even Bonnerjee.

Foreign names, in particular, can be quite complicated both in spelling and pronunciation. However, whatever the circumstances may be, misspelling and mispronunciation are unpardonable lapses.

Once, a British newspaper referred to Mr T.T. Krishnamachari, a former Indian Finance Minister, as Mr Krishna Machari, possibly in the belief that it was a name like Krishna Menon.

South Indian names, in particular, because of their length, provide difficulties for foreigners. Sometimes, a name appears to be a number of separate ones—as, for instance, Rajagopalachari, which resulted in a serious *faux pas* over Radio Berlin in the Second World War. 'C.R.' was one of the nationalist leaders who were imprisoned during the 'Quit India' campaign. This arrest provided the Germans a handy stick with which to beat Britain and so Radio Berlin was quick in announcing that India was seething with discontent against British 'tyranny', so much so that even the Indian princes had risen in revolt. In consequence, the British had arrested their chief, the Raja of Gopalachari.

For at least one ambassador, the strangeness of a name resulted in the failure of his mission. The unfortunate Mr Gluck could not pronounce the name of the Prime Minister of Sri Lanka, to which country he was about to present his credentials as U.S. Ambassador. At that time, Sri Lanka's Prime Minister was Mr S.W.R.D. Bandaranaike.

A common shortcoming is that letters are not answered fully. As a result, the man at the other end has to write again, only to receive a partial reply. Hence the need to write a series of letters for eliciting all the required information.

Letter-writing, whether for business or for friendly intercourse, is an art. To be able to write good, effective letters, one has to have a good command of the language concerned. For that reason, the standard manuals of instruction are of little help. A large business house in Kolkata made a bold experiment some years ago. It employed a man skilled in writing good English to instruct its executives. That practice should be adopted on a wider scale.

Well-written, effective letters could reduce the pressure on the secretary's time and yield better returns as well. Attention has to be paid not only to the letterhead one uses, to the paper on which the letterhead is printed, and to the language of the letter, but also to the typing and its style.

In India, typewriters are used even when they are well past their normal life span. Compare a letter from even a small concern in the USA or the UK with one from an Indian firm of comparable size and see the difference. Many people do not understand the function of a letterhead and use it as a continuation sheet as well. Letters are 'ambassadors', but here this 'diplomatic service' needs to be overhauled totally in the interest of commercial and general prosperity.

Friendly relations are quite different from formal, impersonal ones. Whereas the former conduce to harmony and pleasantness, the latter result in isolation and neglect. There is no reason why relations between humans cannot be friendlier, even though such contacts and communication may be for business and official purposes.

Of course, the large business houses are aware of the importance of public relations, and have entire departments for the promotion of cordiality with the widest segment of the public. But the small units, whose numbers are enormous and keep multiplying with astounding rapidity, appear to be totally in the dark about the value of the personal approach. They seem to be convinced that people who do not belong to their circle of close friends have no right to expect friendliness in what may be purely business or official relations.

It is true that the larger establishments, business and otherwise, have the funds for promoting public relations, whereas the smaller ones have to struggle for an existence. It is a pity that Dale Carnegie's *How To Win Friends And Influence People* is not in wider circulation in the country. This useful book could be of inestimable advantage to the masses because it is a compendium of practical psychology. It is a greater pity that this eminently useful manual on public relations for individuals has not been translated into the Indian languages. A study of this book alone would help the public in general and small business enterprises in particular to attain much greater success than what they may enjoy.

One hint alone could serve as a passport to success—the sanctity of names and how much they are loved by their possessors.

It is true that some organizations stipulate clearly that correspondence should be addressed to the organization and not to any individual in it. This is because when a letter is addressed to an individual, courtesy dictates that it cannot be opened by anybody else, and individuals are not permanent fixtures in any office. Thus an important letter addressed to a man who may have retired or left an organization, could result in serious delay and even loss of business. But even so, such rules do not preclude the promotion of personal relations.

Indeed, since India is a country of small business, and not of big business of the American variety, it would be helpful if the Government and chambers of commerce could propagate the rudiments of psychology which is so basic a component of public relations.

In these days of a shrinking world, as a result of faster transport and speedier communications, we are perforce compelled to do a considerable amount of letter-writing. Therefore, the ability to write a letter is almost as important as the ability to speak. But this is a neglected aspect and deserves greater attention than it is given.

Oddly, business men at the lowest level in the country—the common roadside vendors—appear to be well versed in not only practical psychology, but in the niceties of public relations as well, even though they may not be literate. In the large cities, these tradesmen are shrewd enough to adapt their salutation to suit the nationality and idiosyncrasies of a prospective customer. They are quick in offering the civilities and courtesies expected by customers, but denied by the small business establishments.

Broadly, it is a safe assertion that if we treated everybody, with whom we may be brought into contact, as human beings, and not as robots and inanimate objects, we would automatically build better relations and attain greater success.

A biographer says: 'Andrew Carnegie paid Charles Schwab a million dollars a year largely because of his ability to deal with people. When asked his secret, Schwab said, "The way to develop the best that is in a man is by appreciation and encouragement. There is nothing else that so kills the ambitions of a man as criticism from his superiors. I never criticize anyone. I believe in giving a man incentive to work. So I am anxious to praise but loathe to find fault. If I like anything I am hearty in my appreciation and lavish in my praise" '.

To cultivate the art of successful inter-personal relations, we have to groom ourselves in courtesy, etiquette and cultural mores.

Lack of this equipment can result in racial riots, as has happened in the U.K. between people of different ethnic origins.

Smoother communication helps to smoothen relations in general with everybody with whom we are brought in contact.

12

Your Language and Expression

'The individual's whole experience is built upon the plan of his language.'

Francis Bacon

What distinguishes humans from other living creatures is the faculty of speech. And what distinguishes more advanced people from their less advanced brothers is the wealth of vocabulary.

As long back as 2,500 years ago, Confucius was so highly conscious of the importance of correct speech that he wrote a long treatise, in which he warned his disciples that if they were careless in their use of words, as also about spelling and punctuation, serious misunderstandings could arise, resulting in huge commercial losses and even wars.

In this age of vaunted technological advancement, we pay scant attention to words—their spelling, precise meaning and pronunciation—and to articulation, intonation, accent and delivery. Although we enjoy the gift of speech, we speak and write incomprehensibly. If we fail to be comprehensible, the faculty of speech becomes meaningless.

To standardize and promote the development of a language, we have the facility of dictionaries. Happily, a distinctive characteristic of the English language is its seemingly unlimited flexibility and propensity for adaptability. Almost every word can be spelt and pronounced in different ways. Syntax and grammar, too, are free from rigidity, enabling almost every rule to have a number of exceptions. And as an instance of the adaptability of the English language, it might be mentioned that it has incorporated at least 4,000 words from Indian languages. In consequence, English is indeed 'a language for all seasons' and means all things to all people. When Mahatma Gandhi was asked why he was so fanatically opposed to English, and thought it imperative to adopt Hindi as the national language, he replied with his characteristic guilelessness: 'What makes English so dangerous is that it's so very seductive'.

A further apparent disadvantage is that nobody can give a final ruling on disputed meanings, spelling and pronunciation of words on the lines of the Academie Francaise. In France, the Academie Francaise comprises 40 of the country's most distinguished scholars and constitutes a 'tribunal on language' against whose rulings there can be no appeal. For that reason, the Academie's members are known as 'the Forty Immortals'.

But its seeming shortcomings merely serve to enhance the charms of the English language and to make it the piquant dish it is. Despite the absence of a counterpart of the Academie Francaise, it is possible to say who speaks well, and who doesn't, merely from the accent and choice of words. In other words, the language has become the root of a 'caste system', so much so that, some years ago, the Honourable Miss Nancy Mitford wrote a book, dividing words into 'U' and 'Non-U' categories. 'U' words were those used by the 'Upper' classes, and 'Non-U' words, those used by the commonalty. The ancient universities of Oxford and Cambridge are the traditional seats of English (spoken and written) at its best, but, in recent years, the astounding popularity of media such as the cinema and broadcasting have made a considerable contribution to the standardization of the English language, beyond the confines of universities, and to the reduction of the extent of county dialects and accents.

In the light of this background, the importance of a dictionary is manifest.

Every enlightened household and every respectable office should possess a dictionary, and one that is up-to-date and authentic. But, regrettably, in neither place is so indispensable a utility thought necessary.

When we hear or read a new word, we should obviously ascertain its exact meaning from a dictionary. If we fail to do so, we shall remain ignorant of its usage, or use it wrongly by associating it with the context in which we heard it, resulting in misinterpretation. Many people tend to take words for granted and tag on their own personal meanings to them. Indeed, some of us are brazen enough to seize upon a new word, which captures our fancy merely by its sound, or because it is in vogue, and use it in a sense diametrically opposite to what it actually means. Nothing could be more ludicrous and those guilty of this practice expose themselves to the scorn to which they should be deservedly subjected. We run a parallel risk if we ignore a new word, because as a result of that course we limit our vocabulary.

A dictionary has a triple utility—it helps us to know the meaning of words new to us; it tells us how a particular word should be pronounced; and it is a faithful guide for spelling as well. Should we persist in going through life as blatant malapropists, and violators of pronunciation and spelling, we not only evoke the contempt of the *literati,* but are guilty of the far more pernicious offence of debasing language.

Another point that we commonly overlook is that language keeps changing in fashion in the same way as many other things, such as clothes, and coiffures, keep doing so. For that reason, modern English is far removed from its Shakespearian variety, and Chaucer's language is totally foreign and incomprehensible to most of us. Being particularly vigorous and flexible, English perhaps keeps changing faster than most other languages. Words keep acquiring newer and wider connotation and alter in pronunciation and spelling too. Like debased coins and soiled currency notes, words too are withdrawn from circulation altogether when they outgrow their purpose and period. Therefore, we cannot claim to be modern and abreast of the English language if we sprinkle our vocabulary liberally with archaic or obsolete, words.

Of course, radio announcers help to keep us informed about pronunciation, but they—particularly the All India Radio corps—are by no means infallible.

For all these reasons, a good dictionary is a prime necessity. But, astonishingly, many of the largest business houses and chambers of commerce in the country do not think it necessary to invest in one, and blithely continue in their vandalistic course of denuding and eroding the English language. Some otherwise impressively equipped offices do boast dictionaries, but usually the vintage, dog-eared, tattered relics of a bygone age. To consult an out-of-date dictionary is more futile than to go by an old edition of a telephone directory.

Still more lamentable is the arrogance of the opinionated scholar who considers it derogatory ever to consult a dictionary, in the belief that he knows all that is to be known and the dictionary cannot teach him anything. Nothing could be more humiliating for him than to be caught looking at a dictionary. That would be like a judge caught stealing.

Unfortunately, many commercial and other executives, who dictate letters and notes to their stenographers, do not have the time or inclination to check the spelling of tricky words with the help of a dictionary, but prefer to leave the amanuensis to do so. In fact some overworked tycoons, instead of consulting a dictionary when they are uncertain of spelling, find it easier to consult their secretaries, who are expected to be omniscient. As a result, wrong spelling is put into circulation and sometimes becomes entrenched.

When people are not accustomed to consulting a dictionary whenever they are in doubt over spelling, they are not aware of the occasional changes in it. In consequence, many obsolete or discarded forms are still used—to the amusement and dismay of purists.

In a free world of free enterprise, it is not astonishing that there should be various dictionaries, published under different names, by sundry publishers. Here is a further pitfall for the unwary: which dictionary is the most authentic and reliable that he or she should buy?

Lexicography, though a comparatively new science, is becoming increasingly developed and is a far cry from Dr Johnson's days, when the first English dictionary was compiled and stirred a hornets' nest because of its acutely slanted definitions.

According to recognized authorities on the English language, the best dictionaries are those published by Oxford University Press, whose *Oxford English Dictionary,* or what is generally known by its abbreviated name of OED, is widely regarded as the Bible of the English language. Comprising 13 massive volumes with a total of about 16,600 pages. A less exhaustive version is *The Shorter Oxford Dictionary* in two volumes and illustrated. But for the general public, there are *The Concise Oxford Dictionary,* famous all over the world by its abbreviated name of COD, the seventh edition. *The Pocket Oxford Dictionary*; and *The Little Oxford Dictionary,* which is ideal for school children and office secretaries and stenographers. For the adult public, such as men and women in the professions, executives, Government officers, and others who wish to conform to standard usage of English, *The Concise Oxford Dictionary* is unsurpassed as a valuable guide and friend. Its rulings are accepted as pronouncements of a Supreme Court and it has established itself over the past 60-odd years as a standard work of reference.

One reason for the pre-eminence of the Oxford series of dictionaries is that their original editions were edited by the brothers H.W. Fowler and F.G. Fowler, both of whom were virtual Popes of the English language. Fowler's *Modern English Usage* is still regarded as an indispensable companion to the dictionary by the learned.

Of course, people in technical professions must consult their respective specialized dictionaries in addition. For engineers, lawyers and medical personnel in particular, there are elaborate, authentic, technical dictionaries.

Those who favour *Webster's Dictionary* may not be aware that it is an American publication, and therefore pertains to American usage of English in particular. And as is well known, American idiom, orthography, pronunciation and accent are markedly different from their counterparts in the U.K. Moreover, modern American coinages, and slang in particular, are almost incomprehensible in other parts of the world. Some of the more jingoistic Americans go so far as to declare proudly that they do not speak English, but American.

Regional variations are understandable and merely contribute to the overall wealth of so widely spoken a language as English.

But in the interest of accuracy, and to safeguard against the danger of polluting language, let us strive to cultivate the habit of consulting a dictionary as often as we can.

13
Giving and Taking Orders

'Public affairs involve...an understanding of each other and faith in the bonafides of colleagues.'

Pt. Jawaharlal Nehru

People who do not know how to take orders from their seniors are people who do not know how to give orders to their juniors. Discipline is of paramount importance in civilized society. And the more civilized a people, the more disciplined are they.

It is easy to form an idea of people from the manner in which they give orders to their subordinates. Those unaccustomed to positions of authority usually issue 'commands' to their juniors in the manner of a drill-sergeant on the parade ground. And of course we can well imagine what subordinates think of such 'superiors'. On the other hand, those who have long experience in a position of authority are tactful enough to know that juniors are human, imbued with as much dignity, pride, self-respect and sensitivity as themselves—if not more. The mere fact that somebody is in a junior position does not necessarily imply that he is a contemptible creature, unfit to be treated as a human.

Quite clearly, those in positions of authority should not be feared, but admired and respected. Unfortunately, however, we cannot buy respect and admiration in the same way as we buy a suit of clothes. Respect and admiration have to be earned. At the same time, we cannot earn respect and admiration unless we can prove to our juniors that we are definitely superior to them in talent, intellect and executive ability. Those who are appointed in senior positions as a result of nepotism, favouritism or influence, and are not competent enough to prove their efficiency in those positions, do not command the respect of their juniors. This is not a desirable state of affairs, because juniors should look up to an executive—not look down upon him.

When an executive commands the respect and admiration of a junior, he is discreet enough to know that an order to his subordinate should not be made to sound like an order, but like a request—a request that can on no account be disobeyed.

Some upstarts like to impress friends, who call on them, by summoning as many of their juniors as they can and throwing their weight about with them with the most blatant histrionic incapacity. This conduct only evokes the ire of the subordinates, and the contempt of the 'audience'— the visitors.

It is wise never to discomfit juniors in the presence of strangers—howsoever great the provocation. On the other hand, a few words of approbation, when deserved, double in value when expressed in the presence of others.

Here is a pertinent fragment from *The Analects,* a collection of sayings in the Confucian tradition: 'Tzu Chang asked, what must a man do, that he may thereby be fitted to govern the land? The Master said, He must pay attention to the Five Lovely Things and put away from him the Four Ugly Things. Tzu-Chang said, What are they, that you call the Five Lovely Things? The Master said, A gentleman can be courteous without extravagance, can get work out of people without arousing resentment, has longings but is never covetous, is proud but never insolent, inspires awe, but is never ferocious. . .

'Tzu-Chang said, What are they, that you call the Four Ugly Things? The Master said, Putting men to death without having taught them (the right); that is called savagery. Expecting the completion of tasks, without giving due warning; that is called oppression. To be dilatory about giving orders, but to expect absolute punctuality, that is called being a tormentor. And similarly, though meaning to let a man have something, to be grudging about bringing it out from within, that is called behaving like a petty functionary'.

Another point well worth bearing in mind is that friendship or kinship with a senior does not entitle a junior to take advantage of this relationship at the office. Here is an illustration: Two young bachelors, sharing chummery, were employed in the same office, but one was senior in status to the other. Nevertheless, when the junior was late at the office by even a minute, he would always tender his respectful apologies to the senior. Both ate together, drank together and even chased the same women. But at the office, the least lapse on the part of the junior was severely reprimanded by the senior.

In other words, at work, personal relationships have to be forgotten and the strictest possible discipline enforced. In the process, a father may have to censure his son; a husband may have to reprove his wife; brother may have to admonish brother; and even a bosom friend may have to be put on the carpet. An executive cannot afford to be lax. Neither should he be deferential to a junior who may even be his social superior.

In *Pillars of Society,* A.G. Gardiner says: 'Favouritism is the secret of success'—favouritism, that is, for the efficient, not for the personally or socially preferred.

Seniority does not entitle anybody to be rude to a junior. If orders cannot be given in such a manner that they can be carried out efficiently and quickly, the fault clearly lies with their giver, and not their taker.

14

Avoid Splitting Hairs

'Wise living consists perhaps less in acquiring good habits than in acquiring as few habits as possible.'

Eric Hoffer

A barber, accused of a petty offence, was taken to court. The magistrate observed: 'I see from your records that you are a barber by profession'.

The man's vanity wounded, he replied, 'Your Honour, I'm not a barber; I'm a tonsorial artist'!

'Come, come, my man', said the judge testily, 'You're merely splitting hairs!'

Barbers are not the only ones to split hairs. Far too many of us do so and fray nerves. It appears that the three words most difficult to pronounce in any language are, 'I was wrong'. To avoid using these word, we go to the most devious lengths to show that we were not really wrong, but, perhaps, a little inexact.

Shortly after Dr. Samuel Johnson's famous Dictionary had been published, a woman from Plymouth discovered that a certain definition was wrong. She went all the way to London, thinking she would draw out the great lexicographer in an engaging defence of his work. But when the woman called at Dr. Johnson's home, and asked the reason for the error, the Doctor replied: 'Ignorance, madam, pure ignorance', and shut the door in her face.

Far too many of us wait for an opportunity to catch the other person out in a trifling error; and having done so, we gloat over our 'triumph'. I once knew a harried couple who would take almost sadistic delight in contradicting each other before friends. The 'errors' over which they would squabble were of the most insignificant variety, but they would magnify them to such proportions that they appeared to be matters of life and death. Either the husband would find a flaw in his wife's statement, and she would defend herself with all the tenacity of the defenders of Stalingrad, or she would be the Inquisitor-General, with the husband making a last-ditch stand for the sake of some inconsequential inaccuracy. These frequent bickerings eventually led to a rift, and that rift, in a short time, became an unbridgeable gulf.

When we discover an incongruity in somebody's statement, we should be at least discreet enough to allow him to 'save face' by covering his error, howsoever thinly. Why be merciless, and expose his ignorance? At the same time, let us not be petty, and be afraid of having made an error. We are not infallible, and so there is no point in living behind a veil of infallibility. The Pope is said to be infallible, but Cardinal Gibbon, who was American, made a wisecrack on this point. After meeting the Pope, he returned to the U.S.A., and told friends that he had doubts about the Pontiff's infallibility. When asked why he thought so, the Cardinal replied that the Pope kept pronouncing his name as 'Jibbon'.

If we show that we dislike being corrected, people will stop pointing out our errors, and we shall continue to wallow in our ignorance. Not only are many of us averse to correction, but we assume a superior air of knowledge even when we do not have the vaguest idea of what the other person is talking about. A famous man was once asked to what he attributed his genius. His reply was: 'To my lack of shame in asking questions about things I do not know'.

There is far too much bickering, wrangling, and bargaining in life, and if we contributed our share to the diminution of these unfortunate traits, we should help to make life smoother, and more pleasant. Confucius says that the superior man is dignified but does not wrangle.

There is enough wrangling in the political sphere: let us not spread it in the personal one. It merely leads to unhappiness and quarrels that are taken to the law courts. Among the cases before the small causes courts under the jurisdiction of the Calcutta High Court, 29,000 involve less than Rs. 10. We can well imagine what the number for the whole of India must be! By being petty, we land ourselves in expenditure that is disproportionately great and waste our time in the bargain. India is said to be the most litigious country.

All this, of course, springs from pettiness. Defeat of any kind stings our vanity, and we resolve to teach the other person a lesson, howsoever great the cost.

Sometimes, vanity assumes ludicrous proportions. For instance, one of the numerous wives of a former prince was piqued because she received an invitation to a diplomatic reception without the prefix of 'Her Highness' to her name. The card was returned, and the lapse had to be corrected before 'Her Highness' graced the occasion with her presence. There is no end to stories such as this, and it is by no means the most absurd. People seem to forget that true respect cannot be demanded, but must be earned.

It is only people with the barber's mentality who like to preen themselves with high-sounding titles and designations in the mistaken belief that words can increase their personal stature.

15

The Officer's Domain

'Each morning, sees some task begun,
Each evening sees it close;
Something attempted, something done,
Has earned a night's repose.'

Longfellow

Broadly, there are three kinds of people in the world: (a) those who are equipped with knowledge in their heads; (b) those who do not have knowledge stored in their heads, but know exactly where and how to find it; and (c) those who neither have knowledge in their heads nor know where and how to find it. Those in the first category make excellent secretaries and reference assistants; those in the third category merely swell the ranks of the unemployed; but those in the second category make ideal leaders. They are wise enough not to clutter their heads with a mass of facts not always required, but can marshal information from the right repositories at the right moment. At the same time, their heads are channels for a perennial flow of fresh ideas.

Everybody who holds an executive position, or aspires to hold such a position, must therefore see that his or her head is not a warehouse of unwanted facts, but a sparkling fountain of ideas. However, this position does not obtain on a large enough scale in the country, and there are far too many 'reference clerks' masquerading as officers or leaders. In the USSR, Molotov, one of the Communist 'Old Guard', had such a superb memory for facts and figures that Stalin once referred to him as 'the best filing clerk in the Soviet Union'.

Obviously, every officer, or prospective one, should be aware of the ambit of his domain. With that knowledge, it will be possible for him to deploy his energy and time to maximum advantage. But, oddly, I have seen the Managing Director of a private limited company entering letters into a peon's book! When the head of a concern reduces himself to the level of a junior clerk, we can well imagine what progress his company is likely to make.

On the other hand, it should be the object of every executive to complete his work with the maximum dispatch and the minimum expenditure of time, energy and money. Accordingly, he should know how to organize his work, and should be able to pick the right people for the right duties at the right emoluments.

Far too many offices in the country burden themselves with surplus personnel. This point was stressed by Professor Parkinson, author of the famous and oft-quoted law named after him, when he visited India. Surplus personnel merely increase overheads, resulting in diminished profits, and sow the seeds of staff, or labour, unrest.

It does not seem to be generally appreciated that an increasing amount of work can be done by part-time or free-lance personnel, or by personnel employed on an *ad hoc* basis. After all, the flow of routine and other work may not be constant all the year round, for an indefinite number of years. Therefore, extra personnel should be employed only during busy spells. A great deal of work can also be parcelled out very conveniently to free-lance personnel, or organizations, for completion in their own premises. Happily, some of the largest private-sector organizations in the country have turned wise about such an arrangement, and allot a number of jobs to external individuals, or units, with abundantly satisfactory results.

When staff members are employed on a full-time, permanent basis, they merely add to the headaches of the Personnel Department, which has to work out details such as leave, gratuity, bonus, allowances, benefits and numerous other chores.

Many of the smaller organizations in the country strangely, prefer to employ a number of people, each on an extremely small pay, rather than half the number, or less, on double the pay. More personnel merely increase the requirement for furniture, space, and other adjuncts and multiply establishment headaches.

With the same financial outlay, and in the same line of business, different concerns attain varying results, merely depending on the choice of their personnel. Those officers who are not gifted with either imagination or the requisite level of intelligence, still adhere to the old-fashioned yardstick of academic qualifications—and this is particularly true of Governmental organizations—whereas their more enterprising counterparts can pick talent that can be depended upon to yield concrete results in the shortest period.

In other words, the competent officer, or leader, should be able to evaluate a certain job—and also the most suitable hand who can do it in the most suitable manner. Results are what count, and certainly not a long roster of 'academics' with certificates of dubious worth.

When people in executive positions can count on the loyal assistance of personnel of the highest competence, they can give all their attention to their rightful domain—the planning of broad policies and objectives, the attainment of more business, the building of a more efficient organization, and shorter roads to greater overall prosperity.

Manifestly, the good officer should not merely himself be equipped with considerable mental and moral resources, but should also be able to tap these valuable ores in others as well, in the same way as the skilled prospector taps gold. He should be the imaginative captain of the most cohesive team. Most of the world's greatest leaders in any domain have been, and are, supreme connoisseurs of talent.

16

Invest in People

'Labour conquers all things.'

Homer

Well-informed personnel are an undoubted asset in every field of work. Regrettably, however, personnel of this description are distressingly scarce, because of the lack of interest among most employees in keeping themselves well informed. But since it is in the interest of employers—and presumably most of you who read these words will be either employers, or senior enough to be in executive authority to have the best informed and most intelligent personnel, they would do well to groom their staff accordingly.

Many establishments already have reading rooms and libraries for their personnel, but what they do not have is a special period during working hours for all their employees to visit these repositories of knowledge. Unfortunately, the lunch break is not adequate for this purpose. For, although an increasing number of establishments now provide lunch to their staff on the premises, and so prevent loss of time in travelling between office and home for mid-day refreshment, most employees prefer to use the break for exchanging pleasantries and the latest gossip. Therefore, if an extra break was allowed expressly for all to go to the reading room and keep themselves abreast of the world outside their offices and homes, offices would obviously be staffed with better-informed personnel.

Most offices already receive a large number of complimentary copies of newspapers and magazines, and so it should not be difficult for them to set up a reading room, if they do not have one.

This extra break could be utilized for not only reading, but other forms of instruction as well. Educational films could be screened, and talks by specialists on various subjects given. Perhaps, corporate endeavour might help to make these additional features practicable. Chambers of commerce and other comparable bodies could help to set up cinema projection theatres and auditoriums for their members. Moreover, with the introduction of television, mass audio-visual instruction should be increasingly common and instructive.

Similarly, employees should be encouraged to travel during their leave every year. This could be done by offering a subsidy, payable only when an employee leaves the town, in which his office is situated, for a holiday. Some sort of package arrangement could be made with a travel agency for this purpose. Perhaps, a miniature travel agency could be set up in the Personnel Department of the office itself. Travel in foreign countries, too, should be encouraged increasingly to whatever extent may be practicable.

Those employers who cannot encourage their staff to travel abroad, or even all over the country, should have no difficulty in inducing personnel to become familiar with the places of interest at least in the towns or cities in which they work.

Another particularly valuable amenity for counteracting boredom and soothing tense nerves is the relaying of soft recorded music throughout the day. In Europe, this innovation is proving conspicuously effective in improving efficiency. Here again, corporate endeavour could help: A central relaying station could be set up by a chamber of commerce, or a group of offices.

For industrial workers, visual entertainment—with an infusion of instruction—is the most miraculous remedy for incompetence and ignorance.

Since education in India tends to be lamentably stereotyped and functional, the memorizing of standard textbooks, is in alarming vogue, rather than a genuine quest for knowledge. In these circumstances, employers have a greater responsibility for filling the gaps in the education of their personnel. Many employers in the West have set up virtual universities for the instruction of their employers. Moreover, there are a large number of night-schools and reading rooms.

Investment in knowledge can never be a wasteful proposition. If effort was made constantly to improve the general level of efficiency in any establishment, the increased turnover would offset the additional expenditure involved in instituting the suggested amenities many fold.

Where it is not possible to introduce any of these features, personnel could be advised, and helped, to visit regularly the public reading rooms.

It pays to have not only neat and well-maintained offices, but also intelligent, well-groomed staff. After all, an organization's clients and visitors are inclined to form some opinion of it from its general appearance as also from the general level of its personnel.

Inelegant furniture and surroundings result in slipshod work and general untidiness. The modern trend is to do away with heavy wooden furniture, and to use the streamlined, more elegant, tubular variety instead.

Lighting, too, can transform an office from a dingy den into a hall of brightness, where work becomes a pleasure. Factory and office decor is assuming increasing importance, because of its psychological effect on personnel.

Manifestly, if offices could be made more congenial, efficiency would be improved and profits increased. Since office personnel spend more time at work than at home, effort should be made to see that they are as comfortable at their offices as they are in their homes. But in India, unfortunately, many offices and factories do not provide such basic amenities as fans and drinking water for their personnel.

Employers do not, necessarily, have to transform themselves into philanthropists, but they should have no objection to acquiring the virtues of enlightened self-interest.

17

Importance of Correct Briefing

> *'One machine can do the work of fifty ordinary men. No machine can do the work of the extraordinary man.'*
>
> Elebert Hubbard

As Prime Minister of Great Britain during the Second World War, Sir Winston Churchill was famous for his stream of Minutes to his Cabinet colleagues. So precise was he about his exact requirements that he would ask a Minister to report on a certain problem immediately—the Minute would be headed, Action would be indicated. Frequently, even a highly technical matter This Day—and even the size of the expected report was not to cover more than half a typed sheet of foolscap paper.

Here is a typical instance, extracted from Churchill's monumental *The Second World War,* for which he was awarded the Nobel Prize for Literature:

> 'Minute from Prime Minister to Secretary of State for War—4th February 1841: Please see the *Times* of February 4. Is it

really true that a seven-mile cross-country run is enforced upon all in this division, from generals to privates? Does the Army Council think this a good idea? It looks to me rather excessive. A colonel or a general ought not to exhaust himself in trying to compete with young boys running across country seven miles at a time. The duty of officers is no doubt to keep themselves fit, but still more to think for their men, and to take decisions affecting their safety or comfort. Who is the general of this division, and does he run seven miles himself? If so, he may be more useful for football than war. Could Napoleon have run seven miles across country at Austerlitz? Perhaps it was the other fellow he made run. In my experience, based on many years' observation, officers with high athletic qualifications are not usually successful in the higher ranks'.

In consequence, Churchill's Cabinet team always worked like a well-oiled machine, and this close cohesion was largely responsible for complete victory over the Germans.

When instructions to juniors are not given lucidly often effort is wasted in the direction opposite to what is intended. Here is an illustration: The News Editor of a large national daily once asked a woman, who claimed to be an expert on music, to cover a music recital and let him have her critique in 300 words by eight that night. Unfortunately, the woman, howsoever knowledgeable about music, had no idea of journalism and newspaper requirements. She came to the News Room about midnight, greatly distraught because her critique totalled 331 words. She said she had been trying all night to eliminate the 31 surplus words, but had failed. Actually, it was more important that her critique should be received by 8 p.m., so that it would be set early and included in the next morning's town edition than literal adherence to the limit on length.

This sort of misunderstanding is all too common, and the cumulative effect of thousands of such instances, in various walks of life every day, has disastrous repercussions on the national economy.

Often the man issuing instructions assumes that because his full purpose and intentions are clear to him, they are equally so to a junior who may be summoned, and who may be totally ignorant of the exact purpose of any assignment. When he asks a few questions that he may consider relevant, he is told to do as he is asked and not to bother about 'extraneous issues'. As a result, the man's effort is off the mark, or poor, even though he may be of above average intelligence. Had he been told the exact purpose of the assignment, its importance, and given background information, briefly but clearly, he could have done a superb job.

Basically, this sort of muddle-headed briefing results from lack of clarity in the officer's mind, and his inability to impart all relevant details in an orderly fashion. When an assignment is fully understood by the man undertaking it, maybe he can make some improvements and suggest a procedure that might be highly beneficial to the issuing authority.

Many organizations do not take the trouble to acquaint new employees with the complete range of their operations. A newly-recruited man is merely taken to his desk and given his duties, without his being aware whether he is working for a scientific organization or a commercial concern. A youth, recruited as an apprentice sub-editor of the staff of a daily newspaper, after working for a full week, turned to me in bewilderment and asked me with the utmost seriousness: 'I say, what goes on here?'

On the other hand, methodical organizations give new entrants what is known as an 'induction course'. This course gives new employees a 'bird's-eye view' of the entire set-up, its broad objects and plans, and the working of its departments.

Obviously, officers can brief juniors accurately and fully only when they command full knowledge of an assignment. Moreover, almost every organization has to deal with visitors, external suppliers of raw material and equipment, free-lance collaborators, advertising agents, and, maybe, the Press, all of whom have to be fed with the right instructions or information.

I have visited a number of large institutions and industrial organizations, in the course of my professional work, but very rarely have the officers, deputed to show me around, been able to explain the working of the unit concerned in a manner easily comprehensible to a lay outsider such as myself. This difficulty stems from one common shortcoming: the man deputed to accompany a visitor is a specialist from a certain department, with little or no knowledge of the working of the entire organization.

If every employee was thoroughly briefed about an organization's full range of work, the day he joined, he would take an intelligent interest in his work, rather than reduce himself into a performer of routine duties whose importance he did not understand.

Not only should the intelligent officer be aware of the full working of his office, but also its contribution to the field of work concerned and its role in the national economy. When he remains abreast of all this information, he is able to make his contribution to his organizations overall progress.

Regrettably; however, far too many officers—and even heads of organizations—look upon their work as drudgery in the endeavour to earn a livelihood. In consequence, they do nothing to promote the well-being of that particular unit, or to contribute to the progress of the profession, or the industry in which they are employed, and thereby of the country in general.

18

Introspection and Self-Analysis Help

'He who knows himself best esteems himself least.'

H.G. Bohn

At intervals, all of us experience a definite urge to be by ourselves, to take mental stock of ourselves, so to say. This is so in moments of stress, inner conflict, or when we have to make a pivotal decision.

In *The Education of an Amphibian,* Aldous Huxley says: 'In all the activities of life, from the most trivial to the most important, the secret of proficiency lies in the ability to combine two seemingly incompatible states—a state of maximum activity and a state of maximum relaxation. . . That which must be relaxed is the ego and the personal sub-conscious, that which must be active is the vegetative soul and the not-selves which lie beyond it. . .

'...Proficiency in any field comes to those who have learned how to place the resources of their Consciousness at the disposal of the Unconscious. It is no use inhaling unless we are prepared to sweat. And it is no use sweating unless we know how to inhale the life-giving airs that blow from worlds beyond our conscious selfhood...

'...When the conscious will is used to inhibit indulgence in the bad habits which have come to seem natural, when the ego has been induced to refrain from "straining every nerve", from desperately trying to "do something", when the personal subconscious has been induced to release its clutching tensions, the vegetative soul and the intelligences which lie beyond the vegetative soul can be relied upon to perform miracles...'

Mahatma Gandhi was such a firm believer in the efficacy of receding into one's self in the interest of self-appraisal, self-analysis and introspection that he used to fast at regular intervals and observe total silence once a week.

When we are by ourselves, we have an opportunity of engaging in self-analysis and introspection. We can appraise some of our actions. Was I right in snubbing Mr so-and-so when he came to see me? Should I send him a friendly note in expiation of my brusqueness?'

In these 'conferences' with ourselves—our inner selves—we have opportunities of dissecting recent words, actions, decisions and entire courses of action. We are able to be dispassionate and objective.

Should we be assailed by doubts about the wisdom of taking a certain important step, it is wisest to retire to the seclusion of our inner selves and ponder its pros and cons. In this period of mental tranquillity, the knottiest problems unravel themselves and we emerge refreshed and confident. We can disengage ourselves from the inhibitive influence of myths and fetishes, and allow rationality alone to be the dominant factor. In fact, whatever we do should be governed by rationality.

Moments of introspection afford us opportunities to weigh the wisdom of the sages. For instance, Petrarch says: 'Five great enemies to peace inhabit with us: namely, avarice, ambition, envy, anger and pride. If those enemies were to be banished, we should infallibly enjoy perpetual peace'.

Of course, Petrarch uses the word 'ambition' in a derisive sense—when we tend to become too big for our boots, so to say.

Ambition should be a spur to progress and not an offensive weapon with which to harm others.

Moments of introspection should not be transformed into retreats for day-dreaming, despair and uncertainty. Instead, the critical faculties should be in a state of maximum alert. A period of self-analysis is an enquiry into our progress. Are we moving in the right direction? Are we doing the right things? Why did we commit that terrible blunder a few days ago? A mistake should not be repeated. Instead, it should be a lesson and a warning for the future. Life is too short to make the same mistakes twice.

Uncertainties should not be allowed sanctuary. Instead, they should be cleared away like cobwebs.

Benjamin Franklin says: 'The way to wealth is as plain as the way to market. It depends chiefly on two words, industry and frugality; that is, waste neither time nor money; but make the best use of both. Without industry and frugality, nothing will do, and with them everything'.

According to an Arabian proverb, 'A fool may be known by six things: anger, without cause; speech, without profit; change, without progress; enquiry, without object; putting trust in a stranger; and mistaking foes for friends'.

We should be aware of our weaknesses. Because, as Somerset Maugham tells us, 'The only way to be strong is never to surrender to one's weaknesses'. Thus, without knowing our weaknesses, we cannot be strong.

Thomas Carlyle says, 'The greatest of faults, I should say, is to be conscious of none'.

Those who are frightened of making mistakes and lack self-confidence would do well to bear in mind the words of the founder of one of the greatest youth movements the world has known, the Boy Scouts, Lord Baden-Powell: 'A man who never made a mistake never made anything... Pluck and dash have often changed a mistake into a success'.

19

A Step Towards Emancipation

'Personal liberty is the paramount essential to human dignity and human happiness.'

Bulwer Lytton

In this age of freedom and democracy, it is not astonishing that women, too, should wish to breathe the pure fresh air of emancipation. It is true that they have been the victims of male tyranny for long centuries, as a result of which their talents have not been allowed to bloom. Regrettably, we humans have a tendency to place roadblocks in our path and then to bewail our helplessness. With one fourth of the world's population still illiterate and 90 per cent of the literate sector much too fettered by taboos and other impediments of our own creation to be of any constructive utility, we have not even scratched the surface of human potentiality.

But if the males have stifled their own development as a result of their bondage to foolish conventions and prejudices, they have not even allowed women to reach the stage that they themselves have reached. In other words, the human coach lurches along on two, or at most, three wheels. We can well imagine how transformed life would be if we allowed both sexes complete scope for unfettered development to the maximum extent, in their own distinctive ways.

One of the prime reasons why women are leaving the home to seek employment in shops and offices is their urge for economic independence. Absence of this independence means that they are domestic slaves. But an important point to remember is that when a woman marries, she does not, and should not, sell her personal liberty. Nor should she surrender her individuality. Marriage is a fusion of two independent entities, but not an incorporation of one in the other. It is bad enough that a woman loses her name when she marries, but to lose her liberty as well is a grave injury. In Spain, however, should a Senor Perez marry a Senorita Alvarez, he adds his wife's name to his and is known as Senor Alvarezy Perez. That is as it should be.

At the same time, without economic independence, a wife cannot assert her individuality and remain a free partner in a voluntary alliance.

Some women are dedicated to the home and appreciate the importance of remaining in it in its overall interest, even though they are qualified to accept well-paid employment in an office. And since the duties of a housewife are so widespread and time-consuming, the only fair step would be to allow her a remuneration that would be exclusively her own. This allowance would give her the economic independence she would earn by accepting employment outside the home and yet she would still be a housewife. It is certain that this step would make it unnecessary for a large number of women to seek employment outside, and would contribute towards the improvement of homes in general.

Many women do, of course, imagine that they are augmenting the family income by working outside. But an incisive analysis would show that the domestic loss is much greater than the amount earned by the housewife as a junior typist or a salesgirl.

After all, most modern housewives can augment the family income by remaining at home and developing a cottage industry or a handicraft. Moreover, careless and thieving full-time servants could at once be displaced and the overall domestic economy stabilized.

Professor G.M. Carstairs, delivering the fourth Reith Lecture over the B.B.C. some years ago, on The Changing Role of Women, said: 'From the woman's point of view, it is not necessarily an advantage to be pampered. As an instance only, a colleague who has carried out numerous medical surveys in this country tells me that he has observed a suggestive correlation: in those few households which still maintain a retinue of servants, there is a strong tendency for the lady of the house to become an alcoholic'.

In India, by and large, the regrettable truth is that a wife is still looked upon principally as a domestic servant and incubator. As a result, her individuality is killed and she begins to look upon domestic work as sheer drudgery.

Nevertheless, most men are proud of the 'fidelity' of their wives and refer sneeringly to the increasing rate of divorce in the West, where women are comparatively emancipated. But a point they overlook is that in the West, women enjoy a considerable degree of freedom, whereas here the seeming 'fidelity' stems from economic dependence. Surely, it is far better to enjoy a woman's voluntary love and fidelity than to enchain her independence and mistake her enforced 'love' and 'fidelity' for virtues.

I daresay women are the same all over the world and are just as zealous in India about safeguarding their rights and privileges as they are in other parts of the world. Manifestly with increasing literacy, wives will seek corresponding emancipation, and what has happened in the West will happen here as well. But, perhaps, men could be more enlightened and alleviate the difficulties of women who are handicapped by the country's general social and economic backwardness. One way of doing so is to offer housewives confined to the home an exclusive allowance for their valuable services in the home. This would be a handsome gesture and would mitigate the severity of relations between the two sexes.

An alliance of free men and free women is infinitely preferable to that of free men and dependent women. And, assuredly, happy, beautiful homes go to make happy, beautiful countries.

20

The Range of Your Work

> *'Happiness I have discovered, is nearly always a rebound from hard work.'*
>
> David Grayson

If one wishes to do justice to one's role as a housewife, one should be truly versatile. You have an important job and one of infinite variety. There is a world of difference between a home run by servants and one in which the housewife is generalissimo of her bailiwick.

So far as the most mechanical and routine chores are concerned, servants are of undoubted help. They can be dangerous if too much responsibility is delegated to them.

You would do well never to abdicate overall command of your home if you want it to reflect your personality and individuality.

Being a good housewife calls for considerably physical robustness and hardihood. After all, you have to handle a wide variety of duties that can wear you down if you do not have sufficient reserves of stamina and constitutional strength.

Apart from being a cleaner and cook, you have to be Purchasing Officer and laundry-woman, too. As soon as you have babies you will be required to be nursemaid and teacher as well.

But with a little bit of planning and co-ordination, you should be able to take all these duties comfortably in your stride. For instance, a number of domestic servants can be employed on a free-lance basis, instead of on a full-time scale. A sweeper need come only at a fixed time every day. Similarly, it should be possible to secure a dishwasher on this basis. As far as laundering is concerned, more and more people are beginning to do their washing at home, because it is more hygienic and satisfying to do so. Most modern detergents reduce physical effort to the minimum and the ironing alone can be left to a professional laundryman to come and do on a fixed day every week.

Already automatic dish-washing machines and washing machines are being marketed, but it is true that they are still beyond the reach of the average housewife.

Cooking is a job that presents distinct difficulties, but, here again, the obstacles are by no means insuperable and the rewards for culinary virtuosity amply justify the labour. Remember that the highway to a man's heart leads from the stomach.

Professional cooks are completely devoid of knowledge of the rudiments of hygiene. And this is why a housewife who is a good cook is a godsend. Moreover, she can guard against the danger of using adulterated foodstuff, which is regrettably more the rule rather than the exception these days.

Electricity and gas supplies are now available in most towns and so the days of smoky coal stoves seem to be over for most urban housewives at least. Cooking should never be looked upon as a chore, but as one of the greatest of the arts. Improvising recipes and experimenting with new confections should provide the same joy to a housewife that the creation of a symphony brings to a composer.

But it is a distressing fact that domestic cooking is becoming a forgotten art, and most young housewives have a horror of kitchens. Far more reprehensible is the fact that the kitchen in some Indian homes is not as clean as it should be. In the USA, on the other hand, the kitchen has a clinical spotlessness and members of the family often have their meals in it.

Actually, you should have some knowledge of dietetics so as to ensure that the family is having balanced meals and that the calorific intake corresponds with each member's output of energy.

You should also be familiar with the essentials of first aid and nursing. *Cassel's Nursing Dictionary* will be a most useful addition to your small domestic library. Similarly, you would do well to buy a copy of *The Universal Home Doctor* or something similar.

Many housewives, in the small towns in particular, do their own kitchen gardening. This is laudable because it also provides a pleasure all its own.

Flats in large congested cities make gardening quite unthinkable. However, a talent that is in more universal demand is your prowess with needle and thread. Even if you are not an expert dressmaker, you will always have to cope with broken buttons, tears and minor repairs.

The summit of every woman's ambition is to be a mother and that is well nigh a full-time job by itself. Apart from the fulfilment of a basic creative urge, it brings a great responsibility. After all, the adage, 'The hand that rocks the cradle rules the world', is not empty verbiage. For, after the production of children, comes the need to rear them, observe them and teach them. According to psychologists, the most important years of a child's life are the formative ones between the ages of three and five, and those years are spent in close proximity to the mother.

Apart from these fundamental roles, the housewife is at all times a sort of general handywoman. Her functions are unlimited and it would be impudent for an outsider—specially a male—to define them for her. She alone knows the special requirements of her home and how best to meet them.

But with this diversity of work and the importance of its nature, would it be justifiable for any housewife to describe herself as a mere drudge? When somebody asks her what her work is, she should be able to say with the loftiest pride: 'I am running every department of my home and grooming a few children to be the citizens of tomorrow'.

21

When to Relax

'Men tire themselves in pursuit of rest.'

Laurence Sterne

Obviously, our place of work is meant for work and not for relaxation. Nevertheless, it is all too common to hear the words, 'Come and see me at the office', or, 'You haven't been to see me at my office for ages'. These statements give the impression that those who make them so glibly regard the office as some sort of a club where friends can be invited indiscriminately to drop in for a chat.

At the same time, it is equally common to hear people at restaurants, or even on public roads, discussing the complexities of their official work, the foibles of their senior officers, and the blunders their colleagues make, but which they themselves so circumspectly avoid.

In other words, what is happening on a bewilderingly large scale is that people are taking their domestic and other personal problems to the office, and carrying their official ones away from it. This is manifestly a lopsided state of affairs, and results in incompetence and slipshod work at the office, and a heavy headache, or even cardiac trouble, at home. On the other hand, why cannot we concentrate on work during working hours and relax when they are over?

Some people are conscientious to such an extent that this virtue becomes a vice—they take not only bundles of files home in the effort to speed the tempo of their work, but also all the problems and intricacies of official difficulties, which are inflicted on the family during mealtime and whenever else possible. These apparent gluttons for work grow old and unhealthy, when ordinarily they should be in the prime of life and the pink of health.

Clearly, it doesn't help any employer to saddle his staff with so heavy a burden of work that they never have the time to relax. And it is equally futile for employees to give the impression that they are being overworked at the office by taking home papers that could well have been dealt with at the office itself within the routine working hours. There is little point in their subterfuge to impress their employers with their zeal and their families with their onerous official responsibilities.

If time and energy were to be judiciously employed and attention to various activities not allowed to spill over, there would be a greater measure of competence and consequent prosperity in the country as a whole, as also a happier and healthier population.

There should be no need to work overtime without payment, or to take work home if we gave our full attention to our official duties and worked with all our gusto during the official working hours.

Having given our work our concentrated effort during the full period of the official day, we owe a duty to ourselves and our families—to relax.

How to relax is just as important as how we work.

If we choose the right mode, which varies according to individual taste, aptitude and propensity, we refresh and recreate the mind to render it fit for the next day's work. If the form of recreation we choose is not appropriate to our temperament and is not able to refresh our minds sufficiently, we suffer from fatigue, listlessness and a sense of boredom. Obviously, the form of recreation chosen should stimulate and refresh. A day of sustained and concentrated work, followed by a recreative session, naturally enables us to enjoy a period of deep sleep and to awaken renewed and refreshed.

All the world's greatest people attribute their ability to measure up to their responsibilities to their choice of a suitable form of recreation. Mr. Edward Heath, a former Prime Minister of the U.K., for instance, is so adept at the piano that he once accompanied Mr. Yehudi Menuhin, acclaimed as the world's greatest violinist. A rare tribute was paid to Mr. Heath's musical virtuosity when he was asked to conduct the London Symphony Orchestra. Professor Albert Einstein, too, found solace in music in his moments of leisure, and was a violinist of no mean calibre. Sir Winston Churchill used to go to bed with a detective thriller—usually one by Agatha Christie.

Not only is it important for us to know when to relax, but also how to relax.

22

A Sense of Humour Eases Our Jolts

'The only thing worth having in an earthly existence is a sense of humour.'

Lincoln Steffens

Our journey through life is a ride in a bullock-cart along a heavily rutted village road. Ups and downs are inescapable, but a sense of humour helps to lubricate the axis on which this globe of ours spins.

According to Samuel Taylor Coleridge, 'No mind is thoroughly well organized that is deficient in a sense of humour'.

Samuel Butler The Younger says: 'A sense of humour keen enough to show a man his own absurdities will keep him from tie; commission of all sins, or nearly all save those that are worth committing.'

Indeed, humour is an index of civilization—the richer the civilization, the higher the level of humour.

Charlie Chaplin says in *Autobiography:* 'it is paradoxical that tragedy stimulates the spirit of ridicule; because ridicule, I suppose, is an attitude of defiance: we must laugh in the face of our helplessness against the forces of nature—or go insane'.

Deep tragedy is indeed the best raw material for comedy, and most of the world's foremost comedians have turned to humour as a profession merely to conceal their own sorrow.

Oddly, however, Indians as a whole are not gifted with a particularly high sense of humour. The Bengalese, however, are exceptions, so much so that they have been dubbed 'The Irish of the East'. Interestingly, they also enjoy a high level of civilization, which includes a rich literature.

Sir Walter Scott says: 'What an ornament and safeguard is Humour! Far better than wit for a poet and writer. It is a genius itself and so defends from the insanities'.

In other words, humour helps to lighten our load through life. In view of its many virtues, it is worth cultivating a sense of humour. Why cannot we learn to laugh a little more than we do?

Laughter is good for the health as well. This is evident from the saying, 'Laugh and grow fat'.

The late Noel Barwell, one of the most brilliant British lawyers to practise in India, is still remembered by senior jurists in the country. In his fascinating book of memoirs, he says that in a divorce case, he was finding it difficult to make headway. Barwell was the counsel for a man whose wife was suing for divorce because of his 'infidelity'.

Barwell quoted Byron's famous lines:

'What men call gallantry and Gods adultery.
Is much more common when the climate's sultry'.

The judge smiled acquiescence, and Barwell won the case.

Even political complications can be solved with the help of a sense of humour.

When Napoleon Bonaparte was beginning his meteoric ascent to power and was a slim young man with the designation of First Consul, he happened to ride past a rabble that was being harangued by a fishwife of gargantuan girth. She was inciting her listeners to rise in revolt against the Government's apathy to their misery.

'What do our rulers care', she said with hyperbolic rhetoric, 'so long as they grow fat?'

Napoleon dismounted from his horse, climbed the rostrum, and, standing beside the Amazonian fishwife, asked: 'Pray, madame, who is fatter—you or I?'

The mob dissolved in laughter.

Awkward questions, too, lose their sting when answered with a touch of humour. For instance, the English antipathy to the Irish, stemming from the latter's demand for home rule, led the Duke of Wellington to be cautious when somebody in London once asked him if it was true that he was born in Dublin.

'Not everyone born in a stable is a horse', replied the famous hero of Waterloo coolly.

On another occasion, a stranger, obviously to discomfit the Duke, went up to him and said: 'Mr. Jones, I, believe'.

Wellington replied icily: 'If you can believe that, you can believe anything'.

Here, degrees are at such a premium that people think nothing of buying them, when they do not succeed by cheating at examinations. In the U.K., after Sir Walter Scott had attained considerable fame as a poet and novelist, he visited his old school one day. In one of the classrooms he entered, he asked the master to introduce him to the boy who came last. When a boy was pointed out, Sir Walter Scott called him and gave the frightened youngster a pound note, saying, 'Here, boy, take this for keeping my seat warm'.

Learn to laugh at yourself. It does no harm. On the other hand, it does an enormous extent of good.

During the fierce battle of Britain in the Second World War, when German bombers used to blacken the London sky day after day, it was the Cockney sense of humour that kept hope burning bright in every breast.

Well does Ernest Hemingway says: 'Man can be destroyed, but never vanquished'.

23

Don't Lose Your Temper

> *'A tart temper never mellows with age, and a sharp tongue is the only edged tool that grows keener with constant use.'*
>
> Washington Irving

Lost tempers lead to hot words. Hot words lead to violence. Violence has a variety of forms. Apart from flying at one another's throats, people tend to use whatever implements are handy as weapons of offence—and defence. Easy access to knives, steel rods, and sharp metallic implements results in murder. If the antagonists belong to different ethnic communities, or profess different religions, a communal riot soon breaks out, resulting in heavy loss of life and public property.

People in India are said to have a low flash-point. The more civilized a people, the higher is the flash-point. This is because, it is easier for the more civilized man to see the other man's point of view. Disputes arise because of misunderstanding. The more understanding a man, the easier is it for him to keep his temper in check. In a dispute, both sides are partly right and partly wrong. A dispute arises because both parties think they are absolutely right and the other side is absolutely wrong. If that was true, there could be no dispute unless one or both parties were mentally unsound.

There is a tendency to use abusive words even when there is no provocation. Most of us use such words as a sort of verbal excretion. As we all know, any excretory function gives pleasure. Many so-called abusive words are really swear-words and therefore innocuous. In earlier days, it used to be common to reinforce a statement by swearing 'on my father', 'on God' and so on. In England, before King Henry VIII severed relations with the Pope in Rome, and the country was still Roman Catholic, it was not unusual for people to swear by the Virgin Mary, commonly referred to as 'Our Lady'. Some people would try to back up an affirmation by saying 'By the blood of our Lady'. This oath was soon contracted to a portmanteau word, 'bloody'. Now the word is regarded as an abuse, even though it has a religious origin and is harmless.

It is also true that people in India are unduly sensitive. For this reason, when the country was under British rule British military officers were given strict instructions not to use the usual military swear-words to Indian officers and other ranks. However, British other ranks were subjected to extremely foul language, which they took in their stride. They knew that the seemingly offensive words were not to be interpreted literally.

There is a general acceptance that harsh words break no bones. Moreover, aspersions on the legitimacy of our birth are not meant to be taken seriously. We know that when somebody calls us 'bastard', he cannot transform our birth into an illegitimate one.

We would lose our temper less frequently if we learnt to put ourselves in the offending person's shoes more often.

Usually, the less civilized one is, the greater is his need to resort to verbal excretion in the form of abuse. When we ascend in civilization, we learn to discipline our bodies, minds and speech and stand in less need to utter abuse merely to relieve the mind.

If all of us kept our tempers in check, there would be fewer riots in the country and public property would be more abundant. The man who loses his temper also loses his rationality, and is clearly the loser in a dispute.

It may not be possible to go through life without ever losing our temper, but those who know how to keep their temper firmly in check certainly live longer.

In these days of frequent power cuts, shortage of basic necessities and the problems of commuting to work in large cities in overcrowded public transport vehicles, provocations are very great indeed. But by losing our temper, we are merely in a little worse state than before.

A sense of humour helps to counteract irritants in daily life.

24

Man Doth Not Live by Bread Alone

'A little commonsense, a little tolerance, a little good humour, and you don't know how comfortable you can make yourself on this planet.'

W. Somerset Maugham

Although the most primitive of human actions, eating can be as graceful as any artistic occupation. Customs vary but their purpose is invariable—to make a routine occasion a pleasing one.

There is a wide gulf between the aboriginal of Odisha who feeds on roots and leaves to assuage his hunger, and the aristocrat in the West End of London who sits at a table with snow-white linen, and uses a diversity of crockery and an array of cutlery. It is interesting to see how an everyday action is lifted from the commonplace to the level of aesthetic ritual. The more highly developed a people, the greater the accent on food.

Some years ago, *The Observer,* London, published a most fascinating article, in its feature, Profile, on a waiter who had served at the leading hotels of Europe for about 40 years. This man waited on almost every celebrity in recent history, and his recollections of the table manners of the great made interesting reading, because a great deal can be learnt of human character from the way people eat. An amusing story told by the waiter concerned the fabulous Lenin—father of the Russian Revolution. The waiter had undisguised contempt for him because, he said, Lenin gobbled his food! Not being a psychologist, he was probably unaware that fast thinkers are usually fast eaters.

But since all of us are not great, we can strive to add a wee bit of grace to an everyday necessity.

Habits are an index to a people's character, and therefore it is interesting that whereas people in India in particular like to eat in the utmost privacy, but have no objection to bathing in public, people in the West usually like to keep the routine of the toilette private, though they have no aversion to eating in public. Both these features reflect forms of modesty, but of the two eating in public is the more vulgar. The other practice merely stems from economic factors.

I am not suggesting that to share a meal with friends, or to eat at a public restaurant is in bad taste. But, nowadays, it is becoming increasingly common to see people munching nuts, or eating fruit, or licking an ice-cream cone on the public street. This is an unpleasant habit that has been brought into vogue by Hollywood films.

When the peasant in India sits in a corner of his home and eats his frugal meal, facing the wall, he does so because he wishes to relish his food in private. To do so in public would arouse the desire for food among people who were not eating. In other words, it would be tantamount to eating in the presence of others and not offering them anything. More than that, it would amount to a feeling of 'See what I've got, and you haven't!'

It would be wrong to generalize on details of table manners, because there is no standard form. In fact, what is considered good manners among certain people is thought to be the height of bad manners by others. For instance, a belch is always considered to be bad form in the West, because of its unpleasant sound, but among orthodox sections in India, it is an essential requisite at mealtime. Absence of it leads the host to believe that the cuisine has not been fully appreciated. But sophisticated people throughout the world are becoming increasingly aware of the ugliness of various sounds emitted by the human body.

Likewise, to make a variety of sounds in the mouth, or lower down in the throat, while eating or drinking, is equally unaesthetic. A widespread practice is to talk with food in the mouth, which is a most unpleasant habit. From this aspect, the peasant in India, who eats in silence, emerges with great credit.

A small aid seldom provided at formal meals is a menu. This would greatly help guests in regulating their helping of the various courses. Often we have exhausted all capacity for the multitude of subsequent dishes. Consequently, the earlier ones run short, and the later ones remain barely touched. Menu cards would solve this problem very easily.

Many people find themselves in difficulty at a formal Western meal because of the array of cutlery. It would be useful if they remembered that knives and forks are arranged in such a manner that they can be used from the outer extremes, and progress is made, obviously, inwards, in regular stages.

Food has its own terminology, and so it would be pertinent to correct a widespread misapprehension among people who talk of 'drinking' soup. Soup is eaten and not drunk. It is eaten with a spoon.

Conversation at table should be as pleasant as possible to aid the digestive juices. But there are many people who are eager to relate blood-curdling stories, or describe the insanitation of their localities or loathsome diseases, which would make us blench even if we were not sitting down to eat. Table talk is an art in itself, and it seems a pity that the good after-dinner speaker is fast disappearing.

Sometimes, we have to use the utmost caution in steering conversation with the complete stranger who might be placed alongside us at a formal meal.

With increasing prosperity and a rising standard of living, the art of eating is once again assuming the importance it had in the spacious days of ancient Greece and Rome. But it is also true that 'Man doth not live by bread alone'.

25

The Art of Conversation

'In my opinion, the most fruitful and natural play of the mind is conversation.'

Montaigne

The art of conversation, they say, is dead. This is understandable. With formidable agencies such as cinema, radio, television and swifter communications, not only is the spoken word at a discount, but the tempo of life is becoming increasingly so rapid that some people have little chance of talking to members of their own household.

A story is told of a newspaper sub-editor, whose wife was a nurse, that they seldom saw each other. One week he would be on day duty, and his wife on night shift, and the next week the arrangement was reversed. Therefore, 'conversation' was reduced to hasty scrawls on odd scraps of paper!

If modern conditions can desiccate family life so heartlessly, is it any wonder that we are conversationally barren when we are able to snatch a few moments with our friends. The ancients could hold conversational soirees for days without their outpourings palling on listeners, but, nowadays, a good conversationalist is a rarity. Moreover, the social stream is full of people of such startling diversity that we have to guard against all manner of shoals and rapids.

Social occasions are racially so conglomerate that adverse criticism of communities or races can eternally damn the author in the eyes of people belonging to the disparaged set.

There was the interesting case of an unrestrained young man who made his gambit at a party in Delhi by proclaiming that community X appeared to be as much despised in India as the Jews were in Europe. This astonishing comment drew spontaneous inquiries of, 'What makes you think so?' from two guests—one belonged to community X and the other was a Jew! Therefore, the moral is: avoid statements involving racial obloquy. Speedier communications are bringing the people of the world closer, and consequently in some of the bigger towns and cities, at a party of six people, the guests may represent six nationalities. And increasing international contact is reducing national distinctiveness in facial features.

In like manner, seemingly harmless humour may cause discomfort. For instance, stories about the conversational difficulties of two stammerers are not very kind to someone in the group, who, unknown to the narrator, may have an impediment in speech. Usually it is kind and, wise to avoid criticism, or so-called jokes, involving physical infirmities. Humour is an index of a nation's civilization and is subject to evolution. This being so, stories deriving fun from the embarrassment of the crippled, the deformed, and the infirm are clearly at the bottom rung of the evolutionary ladder. It has often pained and astonished me why even the supposedly intelligent laugh so indiscreetly at the antics of the mentally diseased. Would they be equally callous to laugh at the helplessness of those who are ill physically?

Another habit very common in India, and which originates more from naivety than from the desire to be rude, is the practice of asking intensely personal questions. I once had the misfortune of losing my way in a large city, and sought the aid of a local pedestrian. By the time he had guided me to the correct street, he had taken complete inventory of where I was working, what salary I was drawing, my matrimonial position, what I ate, how often I ate, and a host of other intimate details!

Almost equal to the annoyance caused by personal questions is the revulsion to irresponsible gossip. It is not very manly to criticize somebody behind his back maliciously, and those who think they can become popular by doing so would be rudely awakened to hear what was said behind their backs by the very people who had been such interested listeners a moment before. But, to quote Oscar Wilde, 'The proletariat always talks about the aristocracy. The aristocracy has no time to talk about the proletariat'.

To some, this must appear very dismal indeed. Added to the subjects conventionally taboo, religion and politics, the proscribed list grows longer with the advice to avoid racial condemnation, questionable humour, personal questions, and malicious gossip.

But if we are so bankrupt in ideas that we cannot converse without running into troubled waters, the best course would be to replenish our mental reservoir by sitting at home with a good book. It has the double value that it cannot talk back!

To the beatitudes, I would add: 'Blessed are the conversationally discreet, for unto them will be open the doors of the social kingdom'.

26

Minding Your Own Business

'That which is everybody's business is nobody's business.'
Izaak Walton

Were a Frenchman to tenant a house in a new locality, it would not take him longer than a day to know not only all about his next-door neighbours, but also much about everybody living along the entire street. An Englishman, on the other hand, may spend his entire life in a particular house without knowing his next-door neighbour's name! This is not merely an illustration of national difference in character, but of the difference between two distinct types of people.

Good neighbourliness is all to the good, but undue curiosity about the private affairs of other people does not indicate a very healthy mind. In Taiwan, recently, riots broke out because an American is reported to have shot a Chinese civilian dead for peeping at his wife. If the report is correct, this is a concrete variation of the saying 'curiosity killed the cat'.

It would be both wise and discreet for all of us to mind our own business. In these days of stress, we should ordinarily have our hands full with our own problems. But there are some people who derive vicarious pleasure from their neighbours' difficulties. Not only do they go out of their way to explore their neighbours' discomfiture, but some stoop low enough even to listen to servants' irresponsible gossip.

Rationality surely dictates that we first put our own house in order. But, judged by the trend of events, it appears that rationality is fragile, and invariably an easy casualty.

Undoubtedly, it is flattering when so much external interest is focused on us, and all manner of devices are used to spy on our most intimate affairs, but it wears us down, and is obnoxious in the extreme.

Strangely, newspapers in some countries make it a point of their business to spy on the domestic trifles of the so-called great, and to publish lurid reports on the flimsiest of material evidence. Royalty has suffered much at the hands of 'news-hounds' of this type, and has often protested. However, since most of us do not happen to be royal, we are not affected to that degree. Our problems are comparatively trivial. But the little pricks in life are often the most exasperating.

Correspondence is sacred, and thus it is quite wrong to try to read other people's letters, or to attempt to obtain knowledge of their contents through various subterfuges. This is a point that should be stressed at school, but is not. Consequently, fairly well-meaning people are piqued if their friends are not willing to divulge the contents of their private letters. Apparently, some people believe that private letters are community ones. Sometimes, letters addressed to another party are opened by us through genuine error. If this is done, it would be unfair to make use of the contents.

Similarly, there are people who think they have a right to enter another person's house as though it were their own property. The saying, 'An Englishman's house is his castle' is common, and should be applied to everyone, irrespective of nationality. Although there are doorbells, and other contrivances, some people are persistent enough to ignore these guardians of our privacy, and to stride in unannounced. In these days of housing shortage, many of us have to make do with a mere room. But whether it is only a room or a flat, the rules of privacy are invariable.

In the last resort, our civilization is judged not by the number of sleek motor cars or aeroplanes, or other complex adjuncts of modernity we possess, but by our conduct. By this yardstick, an Arab poem, of which the translation is given here, is refreshing evidence of the high level of civilization that once pervaded Eastern lands—a level that is fast falling under the impact of pseudo-Westernization:

'If you are tempted to reveal
    A tale to you someone has told
About another, make it pass
    Before you speak, three gates of gold.
These narrow gates: first, 'Is it true?'
    Then, "Is it needful?" in your mind
Give truthful answer. And the next
    Is last and narrowest, "Is it kind?"
And if to reach your lips at last
    It passes through these gateways three,
Then may you tell the tale, nor fear.
    What the result of speech may be.'

27

Don't Live in the Past

'Keep your face to the sunshine and you cannot see the shadow.'
Helen Keller

Most of us have met the man who has lost millions of rupees, numerous houses, and a few factories in some war-torn country. Now he is working as a clerk on a miserable pittance, or as a petty shopkeeper, but loses no opportunity to regale friends with stories of his former affluence. 'If only you had visited my home in Yangoon, some years ago, I would have been able to entertain you befittingly', he says with a look of wistful nostalgia. If even a fraction of the stories we hear were true, many countries must once have been veritable El Dorados. Seldom do we meet a migrant from another country who was not a minor Croesus.

With so great a strain on human credulity, it is only to be expected that those stories are now dismissed as 'refugee' stories. There is little purpose in treating friends to tales of our former glory, howsoever true. In the last resort, we are judged by our present position in society, and if it is not as good as we should like it to be, there is no point in making excuses for it by describing the apocryphal days of our past.

Refugees seem to have a common failing of creating illusionary riches. Unfortunately, we have been subjected to far too many upheavals in recent years, with the result that millions of people have been uprooted, and in many cases their losses have been considerable. But human nature is such that it refuses to give credit to facts that are not substantiated. People cannot believe that power can completely crumble under us, and leave us helpless.

When Christ was in anguish on the cross, the Jewish rabble and the Roman soldiery mocked: 'He saved others, but cannot save himself'. When Lady Emma, Hamilton, the celebrated beauty, was reduced to poverty after having lived in fabulous splendour as the wife of Sir William Hamilton, British Ambassador at Naples, and as the mistress of Lord Nelson, and when she tried to make talk of her plutocratic past to the fishwives at Calais, who were her only cronies, they laughed her to scorn. Their comment was characteristic: 'Go on, tell us another'.

Therefore, if we do not wish to be laughed at behind our backs, we should refrain from comparing our impecunious present with our legendary past. It is true that in some cases the claims are justifiable, and, indeed, understated. But it is not in good taste to talk about our wealth, and our attributes—mental or physical. If these features cannot be appreciated without being stressed, they could not be worth much. It is also true that there are many people of noble lineage who have been reduced to comparative poverty through circumstances. Many of the tonga drivers of Lucknow are legitimate descendants of the Mughal royal houses of Oudh.

Many of us have illustrious ancestors in some way or other, but to use them as 'crutches' for our 'infirmities' is hardly any credit. We should be admired for our own virtues and not for those of a long-forgotten grandfather or great-grandfather.

Conceit of a somewhat similar variety is noticeable in the conversation of youngmen who boast of their female conquests, or of their superior looks. This kind of conversation does not ordinarily create a very favourable impression on intelligent minds. For a change, let others praise us for our Don Juan exploits, our Appollo-like bodies, our Rudolf Valentino good looks, or our overpowering genius. There is a great deal of truth in the somewhat outworn adage, 'self-praise is no recommendation'.

Equally distasteful is the vulgar show of wealth. If some of us have so much money that we do not know what to do with it, good luck to us, but to broadcast the fact is repugnant. In a country such as India, where poverty is more the rule rather than the exception, bombast of this type is all the more glaring. It is annoying and irritating when people tell us how many servants they have, the clothes they have bought but never worn, the caches of gold possessed by their wives, expensive shops they patronize, and the sumptuous dishes under which, their tables groan.

Sometimes, even hospitality is used as an advertisement of the host's wealth, and not as a symbol of friendship and goodwill. I am reminded of the story told about Sa'adi, the famous poet. When he was in Ispahan, once, on a brief visit, he was the guest of a merchant, who was in the habit of treating the poet to the most lavish banquets. But at the end of each of these gastronomical exhibitions, the poet would sigh: 'Ah ! for the Feast of Shiraz!' The host, believing that the poet was not impressed, tried to make the next meal even grander. But Sa'adi, nevertheless, left the table sighing for the 'Feast of Shiraz'. The merchant was much troubled in mind, and kept on trying to heap more and more luxuries on his guest, but to no effect.

Some years later, the merchant happened to be visiting Shiraz, and determined to call on Sa'adi. He discovered that the poet was living in a miserable hovel in a nondescript lane. Thinking he would savour the delicacy of the 'Feast of Shiraz', he remained as Sa'adi's guest. To his amazement, he was offered the coarsest peasant fare. After a few meals of this variety, he found it difficult to contain his curiosity.

'Tell me', he asked the poet, 'when I offered you the choicest food money could buy, why did you always refer nostalgically to the "Feast of Shiraz"? After all, your food is similar to the staple diet of the poorest peasant'.

'Ah, my dear friend', replied the poet, 'I shall explain to you. Your hospitality could last but a month, or a year, or, at the most, a few years. In my case, you can stay with me for the rest of your life, and it will make no difference to me.'

28

Courtesy Wins

'The small courtesies sweeten life, the greater ennoble it.'

Bovee

Speedier communications have combined to contract our globe to such an extent that we can now girdle it in a few days, and can converse with people in the furthermost parts. In consequence, our little tribal walls and fencings are breaking down, and we have perforce to consort with a wide diversity of people.

Not astonishingly, therefore, tribal customs and manners are giving way to a more universal code of conduct. Thus, the more adaptable we are, the closer do we keep to the pace of these fast-changing times, and upon our ability to keep abreast of developments in general depends our overall success.

Manners and customs strange to us, do, of course, excite our bewilderment, but perhaps if we made an elementary study of world history and geography, we should see how mankind evolved slowly and how different sections of our species were kept apart because of geographical barriers; the development of tribalism and the consequent rise of political boundaries; and the difference in speech, manners, dress, religions, and appearance as a result of political and geographical factors.

Before we can make ourselves adaptable, we have to groom ourselves to ease the process. We must begin from the bottom and work upward to attain the best possible results. Some people try to present short-cuts by telling us what to do and what to avoid in our daily life in the form of virtual formulae, or a set of rules.

But, surely, we wish to know what we are doing, and why we are doing so. There is little point in doing things we do not understand, and therefore are pointless. After all, culture and civilization are not ready-made garments that we can buy and wear as we like. Some people do of course attempt to coat themselves with a veneer of 'good manners and social etiquette', but the veneer soon peels. Moreover, artificiality in conduct is despicable, and there is nothing more despicable than a facade of goodwill.

Only business men and diplomats make a profession out of conventional courtesy. We certainly cannot build abiding friendship out of a string of 'good manners' learnt by rote from a standard manual.

What we need to build is understanding—a deep understanding of human ways, and foibles, and difficulties. With understanding of this depth, we shall be more eligible for social intercourse. It does not matter if we do not know the correct set phrase for the occasion, but what we are judged by is the degree of our sincerity. And sincerity can grow only with proper understanding.

Quite clearly, this globe of ours will keep on shrinking with the progress of time—it will certainly not grow more inaccessible. That being so, we are going to be drawn into the company of people from all parts of the world increasingly. And not only is there greater social fusion of peoples hitherto separated by barriers—political, geographical, and others—but this fusion is not to be a temporary feature. It will be a lasting one.

Therefore, our obvious course is to throw open the doors and windows of our minds, and try to imbibe ideas, and knowledge in general, of other parts of the world, and other peoples. To do so successfully, we shall have to shed some of our rigidity and acquire a little elasticity, of mind at least.

We also know that what is one man's meat is another man's poison.

But whatever part of the world people may come from, whatever may be their educational background, they expect a little courtesy from those with whom they come in contact.

Politeness has no language, and just as well. At the same time, it is good to remember that extremes are bad—whether they be of politeness or impoliteness, of courtesy or discourtesy. We should know where to draw a line. No books can teach us how to do so. Our discretion alone can guide us.

Excess of sweetness can result in bitterness. Saccharine is supposed to be the sweetest substance in the world. It is so sweet that it is bitter. Therefore, let us beware! Our overtures of friendship may recoil on us with disastrous consequences.

A safe rule to adopt is never to say or do anything to others that we should not like others to say or to do to us.

Personal cleanliness is a trait that is admired universally. And it is also one that can be adopted without any undue pressure on our purses. It is of vital advantage to us from the viewpoint of self-interest—it is conducive to good health and longevity. And it is also of immense social significance. Bad breath, body odour, and other products of poor hygiene can lose all our friends that our pretty manners win.

Consideration for others is a prime asset. Many of us take inordinate pains to build major social graces, but forget the minor ones. It is the little courtesies in life that lubricate the axis on which this globe of ours spins. To forget to say 'thank you', 'please', and 'I'm sorry', where these expressions are necessary, only sours relations unnecessarily.

We have to learn to discipline not only our speech, but our bodies as well. Only too often do we spray people we are talking to by refusing to shield our mouths when we sneeze. This precaution, is not observed also when we cough or yawn.

Furthermore, it is quite common these days in crowded trams or buses to be prodded by a jutting umbrella, or to have our feet trodden upon without a trace of apology by the perpetrators. This discourtesy only accentuates our physical discomfort.

A friend pleaded innocence in his refusal to say 'Thank you', when somebody extended a courtesy to him, by explaining that in India, people appreciate good acts in their hearts, and do not need to give expression to this appreciation through their lips. Maybe. But this is a fast-moving world and so, regrettably, we do not have the time to see if our gesture of courtesy registers in the beneficiary's heart. When I offer my seat to a lady in a tram, I am happier when she smiles her thanks than when she just scowls and sinks into the vacated seat like a sack of potatoes.

Little courtesies are like leaven: they inflate our sense of euphoria.

29

Dressing Sensibly

'Eat to please thyself, but dress to please others.'

Franklin

Notwithstanding the increasing popularity of hippyism and the trend toward social non-conformism, man is basically a gregarious animal with a deep-rooted respect for social conventions. In view of this truth, some of the statements in the Duke of Bedford's *Book of Snobs* make interesting reading, even though the source from which they have been culled is so repellently named.

The Duke says: 'A head waiter once told me: "I can always tell people by their shoes. People who are only trying to show off and impress you, wear fabulous clothes, but are not prepared to spend a lot on their shoes. A real gentleman always wears first-class shoes".'

That statement seems to support a current series of advertisements in the Press by a manufacturer of shoe polish in which the theme is, 'Funny how some people notice your shoes first'.

It is of course true that shoe's are an index of individual prosperity and respectability to such an extent that their state of wear is taken as a guide to the wearer's financial status. For instance, a man in financial straits is described as down-at-heel.

We drape ourselves in deference not only to our own modesty, but also to that of others. However, not only is drapery itself important, but also its design. Sartorial regimentation would result in shocking drabness—as it does in China, which is dubbed 'The Land of the Blue Ants' (from the colour of the suit that everyone wears). But too much originality is just as shocking, because of its obtrusiveness. To reveal one's body is all right—but at the right place (the sea-beach).

At the same time, we should not surrender our individuality, because it reflects our personality—our true selves. Thus, people with untidy minds are people in untidy clothes.

When we go to the market to buy our clothes, we should know what fabric and what colour suits us best. If we take a good look at ourselves in a full-length mirror, with our critical faculties alert, it will not be difficult to choose the right type of clothes for ourselves. Good tailoring should be preferred to a great variety of clothes that are poorly designed.

According to the Duke, 'You should wear your clothes; never allow your clothes to wear you...The wearer's personality should always be stronger than his clothes'.

Perhaps for that reason, the Americans were not particularly impressed with Mr. Khrushchev, who, they said, did not wear his clothes in the same way as Sir Anthony Eden, later Lord Avon.

And yet Marie Corelli says in her best-seller toward the beginning of this century. *The Sorrows of Satan:* 'It is only the poor and proud who take the trouble to dress well...what matter the coat if the purse be full!'

Proclaimed as one of the best-dressed men in Britain, the Duke of Bedford says: 'As for colours: dark grey, navy blue and black are the only possible colours for a man's suit. Nothing else will really do. Do not go in for green suits and as for brown, it is fatal... Handkerchiefs should not stick out of one's pocket: certainly not flowery or fancy handkerchiefs'.

He goes on to say: 'I think socks are almost as important as shoes—small things may, indeed, be the secret of a well-dressed man.

'Good clothes for a man are the clothes that nobody notices. And the same applies to women, during the day... When men dress too well they are not doing well—like an out-of-work actor'.

Similarly, we should give some thought to the dressing of our hair. Some extremely upright and well-meaning men adopt a type of moustache, or a hair style, that makes them look spivish, and even villainous. If one style does not show them to best advantage, they should change over to another that does. Close friends can guide them and supplement the work of a good mirror.

A woman reporter of the London journal *Time and Tide,* which closed down some years ago, after interviewing Norman Hartnell, said in one of the last issues: 'I asked the man, who besides dressing the Queen, makes clothes for a long list of wealthy, internationally known women, for his golden rules on dress.

'As I expected, they are brief and simple: (1) Dress to be appropriate to the occasion; (2) Be careful in selection of accessories to be worn with the agreed simple dress'.

Women in India have fewer qualms about clothes; because the sari is acknowledged to be the most beautiful piece of drapery. Other costumes, such as the *salwar-kameez,* are almost equally beautiful. But what women need to watch is colour—will a particular colour suit a particular complexion? Some daring styles in *cholis* are being experimented with and the decollate model is gaining currency. But need women show so much of their form and impair their overall beauty?

Indian women working in offices are usually regarded as much too over-dressed. As Nirad C. Chowdhuri rightly says: 'They dress as though they are going to a wedding..... They look like over-decorated Christmas trees'.

Our best guides are well-groomed men and women. What do they wear? And how do they wear their clothes? If we observe such people closely, we shall see that they follow a few very simple rules—simplicity, sobriety in colour schemes, good craftsmanship, and designs that heighten their dignity.

In dress and general sartorial get-up, we need to see what shows to best advantage on others—because it is impossible to see ourselves as others see us—and make the necessary adaptations to suit our individual physiognomy, complexion, and other distinctive features.

Clothes maketh the man—and the woman, too.

30

Time is Money

> *'A man is wise with the wisdom of his time only and ignorant with its ignorance.'*
>
> Henry David Thoreau

Some time ago, I received a most generous invitation to dinner. My prospective host oozed affability, and was insistent that I partake of his hospitality. Accordingly, I asked my landlady not to cook dinner for me on the night of the particular engagement, and called at the flat of my host. But, to my chagrin, I was greeted by a padlocked door. No apology was ever made, and it appears that the host had completely forgotten that he had ever invited anybody to dinner. As no dinner was kept for me at home, I had to content myself with a barmecide feast!

Apart from such forgetfulness being most annoying, it is also not very polite. It shows that the guest is so unimportant that it is unnecessary to honour an appointment, and still less to make an apology. Quite appropriately, the next invitation from the same source is ignored.

Likewise, I have often invited people to a meal, and after undergoing considerable expenditure for a special menu and much trouble, the expected guest has not called. Again, there has been no apology, or a letter of explanation. I was merely expected to wait endlessly for my phantom guest, and to dine in solitude even though the customary hour for dining was long, past. This type of nonchalance is not only expensive on the pocket, but against all canons of good conduct.

Sometimes, expediency dictates that we repeat an invitation to a guest who has ignored a previous one. Fearing he might overlook the next invitation, we make no special preparations. But suddenly he calls, and shows annoyance because he discovers that his visit is not expected. Surely, his previous conduct should be a warning to him that his acceptance of an invitation is doubtful.

Sometimes, there is much ambiguity about engagements. Some friends were piqued because they said they had bought a ticket for me to a Christmas dinner at an expensive club, and I had not bothered to come. Hastily, they had to fill my place by giving a last-minute invitation to another friend. But I had given no definite indication that I would be in a position to attend. If my memory serves me right, I had said that my presence depended on my hours of duty. As it turned out, I was on duty that particular night. If invitations were given and accepted in exact terms, there would be fewer disappointments. Ambiguity merely breeds ill-feeling.

On another occasion, I was invited to lunch by a senior business executive. First, the invitation was conveyed to me vaguely by a colleague, who also had been invited. Later, my host sent me a letter in which the date, the time, and the place were very clearly mentioned. Accordingly, I called at the stipulated time, on the particular date, at the appointed place. But the host was not at home. His bearer wanted to know my business. Sheepishly, I had to explain that I had been invited to lunch. Dutifully, he made me sit down, but it was at least one and a half hours before the host arrived home. He apologized for his delay, saying that he had been kept at the office because of a rush of work. But it is not good form to invite guests to a meal, and then to keep them waiting so unduly long. This, again, indicates lack of respect, even though it may not be intended.

These illustrations merely show that when invitations have been accepted, punctuality on both sides is not only imperative but a courtesy that is much appreciated.

However, it is as bad to be unduly early as it is to be unduly late. The former indiscretion implies that we are a little too eager to partake of the special delicacies; the latter that we do not have much respect for the host, howsoever delectable his cuisine.

Apart from invitations to meals, punctuality is always a virtue, despite what eccentrics might say about the charm of unpunctuality.

In these days, when the tempo of life is so swift, we have little time to waste waiting for unpunctual people, and still less for people who dishonour their appointments.

Likewise, people should not expect us to give them a patient hearing if they call without making an appointment. It does seem an unnecessary formality, but the high pressure of work sometimes makes it vital to see people, for business specially, only by appointment. People who call without making any such arrangement tacitly imply that they do not have much respect for the other person's time, or for their own. Consequently, they are treated with correspondingly little indulgence.

Some years ago, a friend told me an interesting story illustrating the rigidity of punctuality in the U.K. He was a politician and had an appointment at 11 o'clock on a certain day with Mr. Malcolm MacDonald, who was a Secretary of State for Colonies, at that time. My friend called at Mr. MacDonald's office at 10.50 a.m., thinking it would be prudent to be a little early. Mr. MacDonald's secretary showed much astonishment, and protested that the appointment was at 11 a.m. and not 10.50 a.m. The politician felt discomfited and took a stroll and returned about 10.57 a.m. Again, the secretary said that Mr. MacDonald was not, and would not be, in before 11 a.m. Just as the clock was striking 11, the Secretary of State for Colonies strode into his room!

Much time, and thereby money, is lost through unpunctuality. Apart from courtesy and good form, surely we should have some respect for our time.

A crime worse than unpunctuality is the habit of asking somebody to meet us at a restaurant or a street corner, or some other public place, and then to be late. This is most irritating. It is not so galling to wait for a friend either at our own home, or at his, but to be compelled to do so at a street corner, is both humiliating and harrowing.

Not only are people late for appointments, but the large majority are late for work. Probably they delude themselves into believing that arrival at office a few minutes behind time does not matter. Punctuality is not only necessary for discipline, but if all those lost minutes were to be totalled, the loss to the national economy would be appreciated.

Time is money!

31

Understand and Enrich Each Other

'How happy many people would be if they cared about other people's affairs as little as about their own.'

G.C. Lichtenberg

A frequent cause of frustration in the home is the failure of young couples to be *en rapport* with each other. This is basically because the young husband is blissfully ignorant of woman's complex nature and is peeved because she is not a female version of himself. In the film, *My Fair Lady,* Professor Henry Higgins naively asks: 'Why aren't women like us men?' Of course, the answer to that question is provided by Oscar Wilde in *A Woman of No Importance,* where a woman remarks: 'How can a woman be expected to be happy with a man who insists on treating her as if she were a perfectly natural being'.

The truth is that, to quote an American jurist: 'The wisest men can make fools of themselves over women, but the most foolish of women is wise about men'.

This is of course because as Byron says:

'Man's love is of man's life a thing apart,
'Tis woman's whole existence'.

Therefore, the young will have to be a wee bit indulgent with her husband and groom him slowly about the devious ways of her sex. Most women are themselves ignorant of their nature and depend on their intuition for a majority of their decisions.

Although the expression, 'better half' is applied to wives, how many appreciate its accuracy? In *Marriage, Sex and Happiness,* Kenneth Walker says: 'According to Professor A.E. Crew of Edinburgh (referring to an ancient Greek myth) the earth was once peopled by beings who were half-male and half-female. Proud of their independence and of their self-sufficiency they were guilty of hubris or contempt of the Gods, and they rebelled against the latter's rule. Their freedom from all authority was short-lived for, seeing what had happened, Zeus, the father of the Gods, split the rebels down the middle, sundering them into two halves. Then he scattered these halves widely over the surface of the earth, and, according to the Greeks, the severed halves have been searching for one another ever since'.

Thus, even the ancient Greeks were aware of the fact that man and woman complement each other in the same way as positive and negative (proton and electron) do in electricity.

It is important to be fully appreciative of this complementary nature of man and woman if a marriage is to be successful. Alfred Adler says: 'Marriage is a constructive task of two persons, of opposite sex, who are determined to live together in order to relieve and to enrich each other's lives'.

When the young wife truly comprehend the powers latent in her, she will be able to convince her husband of her value as a counsellor and equal 'captain of the ship'. In *Marriage, Sex and Happiness,*

Kenneth Walker says: 'Women are usually more sensitive to other people than men are, "feeling" those with whom they come into contact more than men are capable of "feeling" them. As a result of this sensitivity, a woman is capable of giving a better and much more intimate account of a person whom she has met, by chance, than any man can give. This is partly explained by the fact that whilst men are chiefly interested in ideas women are more interested in people, and it is this which makes them such excellent novelists...

'...different individuals are controlled by different wheels and levers in their physical and their psychological machinery, and that the function which, takes the lead in arriving at some decision is not necessarily the function which is likely to take the lead in the decisions of the other partner...

'... the emotions would appear to play a greater part in the lives of women than they do in the lives of men, but this is by no means a constant feature of the two sexes. When a woman has come to a certain decision through the medium of her emotions it is unreasonable, and also useless, for her husband to dismiss her conclusions merely because she is unable to justify them logically. She "knows" that the decisions she has reached are right for her and this being so her husband may marshal the most brilliant arguments against her conclusions without their having any effect on her... She knows of course that men prefer to move slowly along what they believe to be the more trustworthy road of reason but she is confident that a woman's intuition has the power to fly, like an arrow, straight to the mark'.

Walker goes on to say that woman 'is also a greater expert in the science of personal relationships than is a man and consequently she is often capable of greater understanding than he is'.

With greater awareness of woman's many faculties, the young wife will be able to make a more effective contribution to the success of the three-legged race known as marriage.

And now let me give you a woman's viewpoint on a vital question. Here is what Mrs. Harold Wilson, wife of Britain's former Prime Minister, told Kenneth Harris, of *The Observer,* in an interview: 'I'm all for women having careers ... And if they want to be married, and have children, and go on having their careers, I think that's all right, too. But if they want to be married, whether they have careers or not, they must be wives, and so long as they are wives, they mustn't compete with their husbands, they must help them, not only for the sake of the husbands and the children, but for their own sake as well. As wives and mothers, women can do things which are unique and which are very valuable. There are ways in which women can show love and affection and concern which men can't'.

Housewives are indeed the backroom builders of a nation—and is that so little?

32

The Best Tonics are Free

'One touch of nature makes the whole world kin.'

Shakespeare

If all of us bathed every day, drank at least six glasses of water daily, and breathed correctly, half the doctors of the world would have to change their profession. The best tonics for good health—water, fresh air, sunshine and sleep—have always been provided free of charge by a bounteous Nature. And yet what a large slice or the average human's earnings is eaten away by doctors' bills and patent medicines!

The so-called savages seem to have learnt the secret of Nature's prescription to better advantage than we who boast of a civilization that compels us to spend a goodly portion of our life in attempting to remain fit. With all our vaunted scientific progress, diseases are becoming more and more complex, and, sometimes, undiagnosable. Every year, the pharmacopoeia becomes increasingly cumbrous, without lessening the human burden of woe correspondingly.

It seems strange that whereas people are willing to go to unlimited lengths in clogging their systems with all kinds of drugs, patent medicines, and proprietary tonics, they do not realize that by practising a little cleanliness they can rid themselves of their ills.

There is nothing complex about keeping good health. We must drink as much water or other liquids (alcoholic ones in moderation) as we can. By doing so, we wash ourselves internally. We must bathe every day, as a result of which we clear the pores of the skin, and keep ourselves clean externally. And we should enjoy the fresh air, by breathing correctly, amid plenty of sunshine.

Young men are prepared to torture themselves by lifting heavy weights, and by using sinister-looking devices in their desire to build 'the body beautiful', without paying much heed to the elementary rules mentioned here. The human body is not meant to lift heavy weights—that is the function of a crane!

Another simple, but nonetheless important, requisite is sleep, as it repairs worn-out cells and replenishes lost energy. Late nights are the curse of this age. But the agent by far the most ruinous to our structure is worry. 'Take no thought of the morrow' is a wise adage, if it is applied correctly. Because none of us knows whether tomorrow will ever come. Far better is it to take care of today, which is right here. Moreover, worry never solves a single problem. On the contrary, it converts every problem into an insoluble mess. Good cheer, and a lively sense of humour not only make us more bearable to our fellow humans, but keep us in good repair. Physiology books stress the ill-effects of worry and bad humour at mealtime. 'Laugh and grow fat' is a simple and rational piece of advice.

Another careless habit that costs us much in dental bills and general ill-health is the failure to rinse the mouth after meals. It costs so little in time and labour and nothing financially, and yet by our laziness we are made to pay dearly. We take considerable pains to keep ourselves clean externally, which is not so important as internal cleanliness.

In addition to these primary rules, if we took a little care of our diet, we should be wiser and happier people. More harm is done by over-eating than by underfeeding. I shall not waste time and space in recapitulating the rules about diet, which are taught at school. But it is pertinent to point out that the importance of meat in diet has been somewhat overrated. Its disadvantages are many. It is difficult to digest; its wholesomeness is in grave doubt in the circumstances prevailing in some of the larger towns; its quality in many countries, where animals are neglected and unscientifically fed, is miserably poor; it is inclined to overheat the system; and it is known to prevent longevity. From the purely aesthetic standpoint, there is something repulsive about slicing cows, sheep, and goats, and eating them—a point driven home very well by the late Mr. Bernard Shaw. As evidence of this cruelty, a tour of local slaughter-house is recommended before you turn carnivorous again!

On the other hand, vegetable dishes have overwhelming merits: they are easier to digest and have laxative properties; they are rich in vitamins and mineral content; their freshness or otherwise can be gauged easily; and they cool the system. Moreover, vegetarian diet is known to promote longevity.

An important requirement for good health is exercise. Whatever form is favoured, regular exercise is absolutely essential. Even if we do not play any strenuous game, we can at least go for a brisk walk. Of all exercises, walking is probably the simplest and least expensive. Yet it is depressing to see how little we exercise ourselves even in this aspect, and are ready to climb into some form of conveyance for a distance of a few yards.

In the last resort, it is our outlook on life that affects our health to a large extent. If we could learn to make the most of our limited opportunities with intelligence and good humour, not only would we enjoy good health, but we might be able to live much longer. It is worth reading Bernard Shaw's *Back to Methuselah* to appreciate this point better. But if all of us practiced even a fraction of what is 'preached' here, many doctors would have to spend some sleepless nights thinking of other means of earning a livelihood!

33

Signposts of Happiness

'Happiness grows at our own firesides and is not to be picked in strangers' gardens.'

Douglas Jerrold

Lin Yutang says:

> If you want to be happy for an hour—feast;
> If you want to be happy for a day—marry;
> If you want to be happy forever—be a gardener.

Unfortunately, however, facilities for so aesthetic a pleasure as gardening are becoming increasingly constricted as a result of growing migration from country to town, and decreasing dwelling space in consequence. Moreover, everybody is not gifted with green figures, or horticulturally inclined. It would be wonderful to transform the whole world into a vast garden, but that is, at best, wishful thinking. And wishful thinking, regrettably, cannot waft happiness into everybody's life.

Nevertheless, each one of us is entitled to seek happiness. But what is happiness? Here is a picture of a happy man, according to a definition ascribed to Solon, and approved by Herodotus: 'He is whole of limb, a stranger to disease, free from misfortune, happy in his children, and comely to look upon. If in addition to all this, he ends his life well, he is of a truth the man of whom thou art in search, the man who might rightly be termed happy'.

That definition is quoted by Dr S. Radhakrishnan in his *Eastern Religions and Western Thought,* and it seems to be comprehensive enough. However, this article is not meant to be philosophical abstraction, but down-to-earth realism—it is intended to point to certain concrete signposts.

Solon is unquestionably right about the importance of good health. But the trouble is that most of us create complications for ourselves by worrying overmuch, and contributing to the prosperity of the manufacturers of sleeping tablets. The world's best tonics—water, fresh air, sunshine, and sleep—are free. But we are becoming increasingly addicted to late nights, and, thereby, shortening our lives. Tobacco, too, appears to be the antithesis to the fabled elixir, and some scientists claim to have worked out the proportion in which tobacco reduces longevity—with each cigarette, we blow four minutes of our lives into smoke. Scientists say that meat, too, shortens our lives, because it ejects a toxic substance into our bloodstream. Alcohol, which has food value if consumed in moderation, is a stimulant, and toxic if consumed in excess. But, of course, excess of anything is bad, and the watchword throughout life should be: moderation.

Here, we might as well ask: What is the particular advantage in mere length of life? In *A Writer's Notebook,* Somerset Maugham moans: 'They say that life is short; to those who look back it may seem short enough; but to those who look forward it is horribly long, endless. Sometimes one feels that one cannot endure it. Why cannot one fall asleep and never, never again wake? The thought of living forever is horrible'.

It is true that life can pall if we have no clear-cut plans, ambitious, and purposeful activity. But, surely most of us are curious enough to explore the contents of this planet at least, even if we have no desire to be cosmonauts. Regrettably, however, most of us do not venture out of our home-towns, and fewer venture out of our countries. To see the world obviously requires time.

Here we might argue that if we do not have money, it is not possible to do so many things that produce happiness. But this line of thought is not absolutely correct, because it leads people to go in quest of money primarily, even though the wealthiest are not necessarily the happiest. On the other hand, they are often burdened with the heavy bills of psychiatrists, of doctors, of drug manufacturers, and of tax collectors.

In life, not all of us can do what we like. On the other hand, we have to like what we do. As the Mother Superior advises Kitty Fane in Somerset Maugham's *The Painted Veil:* 'Remember that it is nothing to do your duty, that is demanded of you and is no more meritorious than to wash your hands when they are dirty: the only thing that counts is the love of duty; when duty and love are one, then grace is in you and you will enjoy a happiness which passes all understanding'.

What we fail to do is to map out the course of our lives early enough, as result of which we become like ships without a sailing programme. Most of the unemployed remain in that state not because there are no jobs, but because they are not qualified, or experienced enough, for any job. In other words, they have not specialized. It should be obvious to all of us that this is an age of specialists.

Having mapped out the course of our lives at the right age—before we arrive at adulthood—what is the guarantee that we shall succeed? What is the key to success? The answer to the latter question obviously lies in the lives of the successful. If we study the lives of all the men and women who can lay claim to greatness, we shall find that their only asset was a superabundance of will-power.

That is undoubtedly *the* master-key to success. As Shakespeare says in *Julius Caesar:*

'Men at some time are masters of their fates;
The fault, dear Brutus, is not in our stars,
But in ourselves, that we are underlings'.

With success, we certainly enjoy a measure of happiness. Here again, it is our attitude to life that counts. All of us do not have to, and cannot discover Americas, or go to the Moon. I shall illustrate my point. A common bricklayer was asked what he was doing. He did not say that he was merely laying bricks. Drawing himself up to his full height, he replied proudly that he was building a cathedral.

As Shakespeare says: 'Life is what *you* make it'. The Bible endorses this point of view when it says: 'The kingdom of Heaven is within you'. Philosophy, contrary to popular belief, is not mere abstraction, but a guide to the laws of the universe. And this planet of ours happens to be a part of the universe. But if we wish to remain ignorant of cosmic laws, we can ignore philosophy. In that case, however, why bother about any laws at all?

It would also be wrong to think that the road to happiness is necessarily the road to asceticism. At the same time, an important truism is that we cannot expect to build happiness upon the unhappiness of others. For that reason we have to school ourselves to love our neighbours. That, unfortunately, is not as simple as it sounds. To be able to do so with moderate success, we should study the rudiments of history, geography, economics, psychology, philosophy and sex. Because with that knowledge, we shall have a better appreciation of our neighbour—who he is, and why he is so.

Ignorance of sex alone is so colossal that it embitters the lives of most of us. But that is so vast a subject by itself that I can only mention it in brief. Havelock Ellis and D.H. Lawrence deserve to be studied for a proper understanding of it—the former for his research as a great scientist, and the latter for his poineering work as an Apostle of Love. Here, it is worth noting that the greatest revolution the world has ever known is already upon us—that of women against centuries of male domination and tyranny.

It is a major tragedy of our times that love does not hold its rightful place in our lives. In *The New Machiavelli,* H.G. Wells explodes: 'Power has fallen largely to sterile people who have married for passionless purposes; people whose very deficiency in feeling has left them free to follow ambition and to control affairs; people who, being "beauty blind", do not understand what it is to fall in love or to desire children; people who are almost of necessity averse to this most fundamental aspect of existence'.

Should excess of success inflate our vanity unduly, the best antidote to that malady would be a study of astronomy. When we see the microscopic diminutiveness of our tiny planet in this mighty universe of billions upon billions of similar—and many of them much larger—bodies, the bloated balloon of our conceit will be pricked, surely.

Happiness is an indefinable state of mind, and varies from individual to individual. As Sainte- Beauve says: 'In life, happiness and misery are separated by so small a division, or so slight an event, that this may well be compared to the trembling of a leaf'.

I have tried to compress into capsular form something that requires far more space than this to do it minimum justice. Nevertheless, the quest for happiness is so basic an impulsion in all of us that it is appropriate to say something about it. But those who seem to think that happiness is not possible for anybody, except glamorous film stars, millionaires, and members of royalty, would do well to remember the inspiring words of Baron Pierre de Coubertin, founder of the modern Olympic Games: 'The most important thing in the Olympic Games is not to win, but to take part; just as the most important thing in life is not the triumph but the struggle. The essential thing is not to have conquered, but to have fought well'.

❑❑❑